Low-Acid SLOW COOKING

Low-Acid SLOW COOKING

Over 100 Reflux-Free Recipes for the Electric Slow Cooker

Dominique DeVito

with Breea Johnson, M.S., R.D., L.D.N.

CIDER MILL PRESS

BOOK PUBLISHERS

Kennebunkport, Maine

13-Digit ISBN: 978-1604333176
10-Digit ISBN: 1604333170

This book may be ordered by mail from the publisher. Please include $3.95 for postage and handling.
Please support your local bookseller first!

Books published by Cider Mill Press Book Publishers are available at special discounts for bulk purchases in the United States by corporations, institutions, and other organizations. For more information, please contact the publisher.

Cider Mill Press Book Publishers
"Where good books are ready for press"
12 Port Farm Road
Kennebunkport, Maine 04046

Visit us on the Web!
www.cidermillpress.com

Design by Alicia Freile, Tango Media
Typeset by Candice Fitzgibbons, Tango Media
Typography: Archer, Chaparral Pro, Helvetica Neue and Voluta
All images used under license from Shutterstock.com.
Printed in China

1 2 3 4 5 6 7 8 9 0
First Edition

Contents

Eating to Manage Acid Reflux

*I*f you're picking up this book, you are ready for a change. You're looking for relief from the uncomfortable feelings associated with acid reflux—indigestion, heartburn, and more. When you recognize and can manage the foods and beverages that make the condition worse—and better!—you can start feeling better almost immediately. In addition, you'll learn how much the slow cooker can be your friend. Gather the ingredients, assemble them in the cooker, and go. Delicious and healthy meals will be waiting for you when you are ready for them.

Another significant benefit of slow-cooked meals for sufferers of reflux is that when foods are cooked over long periods of time, it makes them easier to digest overall. Reflux sufferers often have weak digestive systems as a consequence of the condition, and slow-cooked meals are gentle on their systems.

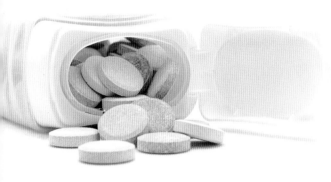

About Acid Reflux

We are all familiar with the numerous advertisements on television for antacids to relieve indigestion, heartburn, and gas—all conditions related to stomach juices coming up the throat. There are lots of ads for these medications, because there are lots of people using them. An article in *USA Today* in 2011 reported, "A recent study found that 1 in 10 people buys an antacid at least once a month. Sales of antacids nationwide jumped 7% in 2010, pulling in $1.2 billion, according to *Drug Store News*, a publication on the pharmaceutical industry."

That's right: Antacids are a billion-dollar industry here in the United States, and growing. With increased research on the subject, it's believed that there's a 50/50 chance that anyone over the age of 40 has some form of acid reflux. The incidence is spreading to younger people, too. And it's afflicting those who are in good shape as well as those who aren't.

The burning and uncomfortable feelings of indigestion and heartburn are only the tip of the iceberg. Reflux can cause many other symptoms, even without the feeling of indigestion.

Do you experience any of the following symptoms regularly?

* Some form of heartburn (chest pain after eating)
* Trouble swallowing
* A chronic cough
* Shortness of breath
* Hoarseness in the morning
* Post-nasal drip

Dr. Jamie Koufman, author of *Dropping Acid: The Reflux Diet Cookbook & Cure*, coined the term "silent reflux" to incorporate many of the symptoms that are commonly associated with asthmas and allergies but are often caused by reflux. It turns out that acid alone isn't the primary culprit. Digestive acid works along with the digestive enzyme pepsin, which is one of many digestive enzymes but which targets the breakdown of proteins. Pepsin can't work without acid, though: When acid is present, pepsin goes to work breaking things down. The thing is, it doesn't matter to pepsin whether its source of acid is coming up from the stomach or down from something being ingested. If it's in the tissues of your throat, voice box, or esophagus, it can be reactivated with any source of acid.

Ultimately, then, if dietary acids are minimized, pepsins have less to work with, and tissue can heal, relieving reflux symptoms. Diet can play a large part in this.

Eating to Manage Acid Reflux

If you want to feel better and experience less reflux, you will need to become familiar with what foods and beverages are okay to consume on a regular basis—and which are not. Remember, too, that everyone is different. If you are doing your best to follow the guidelines in this cookbook and other low-acid resources and you aren't feeling any improvement, there may be something else going on. Work with a trusted medical professional for best results.

Let's cut to the chase: The following list is of foods that should be *avoided*. They are certifiably inappropriate foods for sufferers of reflux. Why? Because they're loaded with acid.

Key offenders:
* Alcoholic beverages (all beer, wine, and spirits)
* Coffee, tea, and other caffeinated (or decaffeinated) beverages; if you can't live without coffee, limit it to no more than 1 cup a day
* All carbonated beverages
* Citrus fruits and juices
* Tomatoes and tomato sauces
* Raw onions and garlic
* Vinegar
* Chocolate (the higher the fat content, the worse it is for you; for example, a milk chocolate will exacerbate reflux more than a lower-fat dark chocolate)
* Fatty meats, including beef, pork sausages, ribs, etc.
* Anything deep-fried
* Hot sauces and hot peppers
* Nuts that are high in fat, such as peanuts, cashews, and walnuts
* Peppermint and spearmint

Offenders that can be used in moderation:
* Butter, margarine, shortening, or lard. These high-fat flavorings are the backbones of so many cooked foods that it is nearly impossible to sustain a diet without them. The key is to use them sparingly as flavorings or for cooking and not to overdo their use.
* High-fat dairy products such as cheese and creams. Try to avoid those with the highest fat content, like whole milk heavy cream, or a cheese like Brie. Finding low- or non-fat substitutes can bring a lot of variety to your meals. Fortunately, there are a lot of choices for these in most supermarkets.
* Eggs. The yolk is the part with the high fat content. Reflux sufferers should abstain from eating whole egg-laden dishes, but one or two on occasion, or as part of a healthy recipe, is acceptable.

Fruits and Vegetables

When the concept of "diet" comes to mind, fruits and vegetables are typically the foods that can be eaten almost limitlessly. Not for sufferers of reflux. Even among a common fruit like the apple, pH (acid) levels vary, making some varieties better than others. It gets confusing. Here's a partial list to help with basic choices. The recipes in the book indicate which varieties are best to select.

* Apples. Those with the lowest pH are Red Delicious, Fuji, and Gala. Granny Smith and Macintosh apples are varieties with higher acid and should be avoided.
* Onions. The white onion is the kind suitable for those who need a low-acid diet. Stay away from yellow or Spanish onions.
* Potatoes. Stick with Idaho and Yukon Gold and you are fine!
* Mushrooms. The best are Portobello and—fortunately—domestic mushrooms. Use others sparingly.
* Peppers. The red, orange, and yellow peppers are lowest in pH, with green peppers and Italian peppers being slightly higher. Stick with the red, orange, and yellow peppers.

Exploring What You *Can* Eat!

The good news is that there are lots of foods that can be eaten in abundance and which provide great satisfaction. Top of the list is grain products: breads, pasta, polenta, rice, couscous, bulgur, quinoa—there are lots of great grains you can eat. As with any diet, the higher the whole grain content, the better. And while you can't slather your breads with high-fat spreads like butter or regular mayonnaise, you can use butter sparingly, and there are many sugar-free jams and more nutritious nut butters (such as almond butter) that are healthy and satisfying.

The foods that are best for those who suffer from reflux are:
* Root vegetables and greens—including cauliflower, broccoli, asparagus, beans, kale, chard, sweet potatoes, and more. Although raw vegetables can sometimes aggravate reflux, when prepared in a slow cooker that breaks down the cell walls, they become ideal foods.
* Chicken and turkey are great low-fat, lean sources of protein—so long as the skin is removed and you do not eat them fried or sautéed in lots of butter or smothered in a rich sauce.
* Fish and seafood—while your selection in this category is large, you want to look for wild fish and not farm-raised fish, and you want to minimize

any processed fish or fish that's been prepared with other fats, like coconut shrimp, for example.

* Grains—Although whole grains are best, reflux isn't aggravated by any grains, so you can eat everything from multi-grain breads to regular bulgur and white rice. There are lots of choices in this category.
* Melon
* Fennel
* Bananas

Dressing Up the Low-Acid Diet

It may seem like sticking to a low-acid diet means giving up the foods that make dishes flavorful and fulfilling. Instead of thinking about what you have to lose, however, consider all the flavors and ingredients you can use to your heart's content. A new world of food may be awaiting you. For example, here are some yummy things you can indulge in:

* Maple syrup and brown sugar
* Parmesan and cheddar cheeses
* 2% milk and low- or non-fat creams (like half-and-half)

* Non-fat yogurt
* Dijon mustard
* Vinaigrette—yes, it's true!
* Low-sodium soy sauce
* Fresh ginger
* The *zest* of lemons and oranges (not the juice or fruit itself)

You'll find that in the recipes in this book we have tried to incorporate as many fun flavorings as possible. Once you become familiar with ingredients you'll need frequently and your pantry is stocked with them, it will become easier and easier to create meals that provide the satisfaction you crave.

Let's get cooking!

Chapter 1

Slow Going:
A Guide to Slow Cookers and the Wonders of Slow Cooking

*L*uckily for all of us who are "science challenged," it doesn't take a degree in physics to operate a slow cooker. It's about the easiest machine there is on the market. It's certainly far less complicated than an espresso machine or even a waffle maker. In this chapter you'll learn about slow cookers and how to get the best results from them.

Slow cookers are inexpensive to operate; they use about as much electricity as a 60-watt bulb. They are also as easy to operate as flipping on a light switch.

Slow cookers operate by cooking food using indirect heat at a Low temperature for an extended period of time. Here's the difference: Direct heat is the power of a stove burner underneath a pot, while indirect heat is the overall heat that surrounds foods as they bake in the oven.

You can purchase a slow cooker for as little as $20 at a discount store, while the top-of-the-line ones sell for more than $200. They all function in the same simple way; what increases the cost is the "bells and whistles" factors. Slow cookers come in both round and oval shapes, but they operate the same regardless of shape.

Food is assembled in a pottery insert that fits inside a metal housing and is topped with a clear lid. The food cooks from the heat generated by the circular heating wires encased between the slow cooker's outer and inner layers of metal. The coils never directly touch the crockery insert. As the element heats, it gently warms the air between the two layers of metal, and it is the hot air that touches the pottery. This construction method eliminates the need for stirring because no part of the pot gets hotter than any other.

On the front of this metal casing is the control knob. All slow cookers have Low and High settings, and most also have a Stay Warm position. Some new machines have a programmable option that enables you to start food on High and then the slow cooker automatically reduces the heat to Low after a programmed time.

The largest variation in slow cookers is their size, which range from tiny 1-quart models that are excellent for hot dips and fondue but fairly useless for anything else to gigantic 7-quart models that are excellent for large families and large batches.

Rival introduced the first slow cooker, the Crock-Pot, in 1971, and the introductory slogan remains true more than 35 years later: It "cooks all day while the cook's away." Like such trademarked names as Kleenex for paper tissue or Formica for plastic laminate, Crock-Pot has almost become synonymous with the slow cooker. However, not all slow cookers are Crock-Pots, so the generic term is used in this book.

Most of the recipes in this book were written for and tested in a 4- or 5-quart slow cooker; that is what is meant by *medium*. Either of those sizes makes enough for four to eight people, depending on the recipe.

Slow Cookers and Food Safety

Questions always arise as to the safety of slow cookers. The Food Safety and Inspection Service of the U.S. Department of Agriculture approves slow cooking as a method for safe food preparation. The lengthy cooking and the steam created within the tightly covered pot combine to destroy any bacteria that might be present in the food. But you do have to be careful.

It's far more common for food-borne illness to start with meat, poultry, and seafood than from contaminated fruits and vegetables. That is why it's not wise to cook whole chickens or cuts of meat larger than those specified in the recipes in this book because during slow cooking, these large items remain too long in the bacterial "danger zone"— between 40°F and 140°F. It is important that food reaches the higher temperature in less than two hours and remains at more than 140°F for at least 30 minutes.

Getting a jump-start on dinner while you're preparing breakfast may seem like a Herculean task, and it is possible to prep the ingredients destined for the slow cooker the night before—with some limitations. If you cut meat or vegetables in advance, store them separately in the refrigerator and layer them in the slow cooker in the morning. However, do not store the cooker insert in the refrigerator because that will

> Always thaw food before placing it in the slow cooker to ensure the trip from 40°F to 140°F is accomplished quickly and efficiently. While adding a package of frozen green beans will slow up the cooking, starting with a frozen pot roast or chicken breast will make it impossible for the Low temperature of the slow cooker to accomplish this task.

also increase the amount of time it takes to heat the food to a temperature that kills bacteria.

Concern about food safety extends to after a meal is cooked and the leftovers are ready for storage. As long as the temperature remains 140°F or higher, food will stay safe for many hours in the slow cooker. Leftovers, however, should never be refrigerated in the crockery insert because it will take them too long to go through the "danger zone" in the other direction—from hot to cold.

Freeze or refrigerate leftovers in shallow containers within two hours after a dish has finished cooking. Also, food should never be reheated in the slow cooker because it takes too long for chilled food to reheat. Bacteria are a problem on cooked food as well as raw ingredients. The slow cooker can be used to keep food warm—and without the fear of burning it—once it has been reheated on the stove or in the oven.

One of the other concerns about food safety and the slow cooker is if there is a loss of power in the house—especially if you don't know when it occurred in the cooking process. If you're home, and the amount of time was minimal, add it back into your end time. If the time without power increases to more than 30 minutes, finish the food by conventional cooking, adding more liquid, if necessary.

However, if you set the slow cooker before you left for work, and realize from electric clocks that power was off for more than an hour, it's best to discard the food, even if it looks done. You have no idea if the power outage occurred before the food passed through the "danger zone." Better safe than sorry.

Slow Cooker Hints

Slow cookers can be perplexing if you're not accustomed to using one. Here are some general tips to help you master slow cooker conundrums:

* Remember that cooking times are wide approximations—within hours rather than minutes! That's because the age or power of a slow cooker as well as the temperature of ingredients must be taken into account. Check the food at the beginning of the stated cooking time, and then gauge whether it needs more time and about how much time. If carrots or cubes of potato are still rock-hard, for example, turn the heat to High if cooking on Low, and realize that you're looking at another hour or so.

* Foods cook faster on the bottom of a slow cooker than at the top because there are more heat coils and they are totally immersed in the simmering liquid.

* Appliance manufacturers say that slow cookers can be left on either High or Low unattended, but use your own judgment. If you're going to be out of the house all day, it's advisable to cook food on Low. If, on the other hand, you're going to be gone for just a few hours, the food will be safe on High.

Many families don't think to use their slow cookers in the summer. But running the slow cooker doesn't raise the kitchen temperature by even a degree, and you can be outside enjoying the warm weather while it's cooking away.

* Use leaf versions of dried herbs such as thyme and rosemary rather than ground versions. Ground herbs tend to lose potency during many hours in the slow cooker.

* Don't add dairy products except at the end of the cooking time, as noted in the recipes. They can curdle if cooked for too long.

* If you want a sauce to have a more intense flavor, you can reduce the liquid in two ways. If cooking on Low, raise the heat to High, and remove the lid for the last hour of cooking. This will achieve some evaporation of the liquid. Or, remove the liquid either with a bulb baster or strain the liquid from the solids, and reduce them in a saucepan on the stove.

Slow Cooker Cautions

Slow cookers are benign, but they are electrical appliances with all the concomitant hazards of any machine plugged into a live wire. Be careful that the cord is not frayed in any way, and plug the slow cooker into an outlet that is not near the sink.

Here are some tips on how to handle them:

* Never leave a slow cooker plugged in when not in use. It's all too easy to accidentally turn it on and not notice until the crockery insert cracks from overheating with nothing in it.

* Conversely, do not preheat the empty insert while you're preparing the food because the insert could crack when you add the cold food.

* Never submerge the metal casing in water or fill it with water. The inside of the metal does occasionally get dirty, but you can clean it quite well with an abrasive cleaner and then wipe it with a damp cloth or paper towel. While it's not aesthetically pleasing to see dirty metal, food never touches it, so if there are a few drips here and there it's not really important.

* Always remember that the insert is fragile, so don't drop it. Also, don't put a hot insert on a cold counter; that could cause it to break, too. The reverse is also true. While you can use the insert as a casserole in a conventional oven (assuming the lid is glass and not plastic), it cannot be put into a preheated oven if chilled.

Modern slow cookers heat slightly hotter than those made thirty years ago; the Low setting on a slow cooker is about 200°F while the High setting is close to 300°F. If you have a vintage appliance, it's a good idea to test it to make sure it still has the power to heat food sufficiently. Leave 2 quarts water at room temperature overnight, and then pour the water into the slow cooker in the morning. Heat it on Low for 8 hours. The temperature should be 185°F after 8 hours. Use an instant read thermometer to judge it. If it is lower, any food you cook in this cooker might not pass through the danger zone rapidly enough.

* Resist the temptation to look and stir. Every time you take the lid off the slow cooker, you need to add 10 minutes of cooking time if cooking on High and 20 minutes if cooking on Low to compensate. Certain recipes in this book, especially those for fish, instruct you to add ingredients during the cooking time. In those cases the heat loss from opening the pot has been factored in to the total cooking time.

* Don't add more liquid to a slow cooker recipe than that specified in the recipe. Even if the food is not submerged in liquid when you start, foods such as meats and vegetables give off liquid as they cook; in the slow cooker, that additional liquid does not evaporate.

High-Altitude Adjustment

Rules for slow cooking, along with all other modes of cooking, change when the slow cooker is located more than 3,000 feet above sea level. At high altitudes the air is thinner so water boils at a lower temperature and comes to a boil more quickly. The rule is to always cook on High when above 3,000 feet; use the Low setting as a Keep Warm setting.

Other compensations are to reduce the liquid in a recipe by a few tablespoons and add about 5 to 10 percent more cooking time. The liquid may be bubbling, but it's not 212°F at first.

Converting Recipes for the Slow Cooker

Once you feel comfortable with your slow cooker, you'll probably want to use it to prepare your favorite recipes you now cook on the stove or in the oven.

The best recipes to convert are wet ones with a lot of liquid, such as stews, soups, chilies, and other braised foods. Not all dishes can be easily converted to slow cooked dishes. Even if a dish calls for liquid, if it's supposed to be cooked or baked uncovered, chances are it will not be successfully transformed to a slow cooker recipe, because the food will not brown and the liquid will not evaporate.

The easiest way to convert your recipes is to find a similar one in this book and use its cooking time for guidance. When looking for a similar recipe, take into account the amount of liquid specified as well as the quantity of food. The liquid transfers the heat from the walls of the insert into the food itself, and the liquid heats in direct proportion to its measure. You should look for similar recipes as well as keep in mind some general guidelines:

* Most any stew or roast takes 6 to 10 hours on Low and 3 to 5 hours on High.
* Chicken dishes cook more rapidly. Count on 6 to 8 hours on Low and 3 to 4 hours on High.
* Quadruple the time from conventional cooking to cooking on Low, and at least double it for cooking on High.
* Cut back on the amount of liquid used in stews by about half. Unlike cooking on the stove or in the oven, there is little to no evaporation in the slow cooker.
* For soups, cut back on the liquid by one-third if the soup is supposed to simmer uncovered, and cut back by one-fourth if the soup is simmered covered. Even when covered, a soup that is simmering on the stove has more evaporation than one cooked in the slow cooker.

Stocking Up

These stocks are referenced in several recipes in this book. Stocks are no more difficult to make than boiling water; all they are is lots of water into which other ingredients simmer for many hours to create water with an enriched flavor.

In the same way that you can use bits of leftover vegetables in soups, many of the vegetables that go into stocks would otherwise end up in the garbage can or compost bin. Save those carrot and onion peeling, parsley stems, the base off a celery stalk, and the dark green scallion tops. All of those foods might not wend their way into cooking a dish, but they're fine for stock!

You can keep different bags in your freezer in anticipation of making stock on a regular basis. Store individual bags for chicken trimmings, shrimp shells, fish skin and bones, and one for vegetables past their prime and their trimmings. When a bag is full, it's time to make stock.

Table of Liquid Measurements

Pinch	=	less than $1/8$ teaspoon
3 teaspoons	=	1 tablespoon
2 tablespoons	=	1 ounces
8 tablespoons	=	$1/2$ cup
2 cups	=	1 pint
1 quart	=	2 pints
1 gallon	=	4 quarts

Once your stock is cooked—and the fat removed from chicken stock—you should freeze it in containers of different sizes. I do about half a batch in heavy, resealable quart bags; they are the basis for soups. Bags take up less room in the freezer than containers. Freeze them flat on a baking sheet and then they can be stacked on a freezer shelf or in the cubbyholes on the freezer door.

Freeze stock in 1-cup measures and some in ice cube trays. Measure the capacity of your ice cube tray with a measuring tablespoon; it will be somewhere between 1 and 3 tablespoons. Keep a bag of stock cubes for those recipes that require just a small amount.

Chicken Stock

Chicken stock is used more than any other stock. It adds a rich flavor to soups not created when using water, and it is used in recipes for pork and veal as well as poultry. You'll see in the variations at the end of this recipe that there are ways to make it more appropriate to various ethnic cuisines too.

Makes 2 quarts | Prep time: 10 minutes | Minimum cook time: 4 hours in a medium slow cooker

2 quarts boiling water

2 pounds chicken pieces
(e.g., bones, skin, wing tips)

1 carrot, cut into ½-inch chunks

1 medium onion, sliced

1 celery rib, sliced

3 parsley sprigs, rinsed

1 tablespoon black peppercorns

3 thyme sprigs, rinsed, or 1 teaspoon dried

1 garlic clove, peeled

1 bay leaf

1. Pour water into the slow cooker. Add chicken pieces, carrot, onion, celery, peppercorns, parsley, thyme, garlic, and bay leaf. Cook on Low for 8 to 10 hours or on High for 4 to 5 hours, or until chicken and vegetables are falling apart.

2. Strain stock through a sieve into a mixing bowl. Press down on solids with the back of a spoon to extract as much liquid as possible. Discard solids.

3. Chill stock. Remove and discard fat layer from top. Ladle stock into containers.

Note: The stock can be refrigerated for up to 4 days, or frozen for up to 6 months.

Variation:

✳ For browner chicken stock: Preheat the oven broiler, and line a broiler pan with heavy-duty aluminum foil. Broil chicken bones for 3 minutes per side, or until browned, and use the browned bones for the stock.

> Starting the time in the slow cooker with the liquid already boiling saves hours of cooking time. This is a tip that can be applied to anything you cook in the slow cooker. To test to see how much time it saves, start a recipe and see how long it takes to come to a boil. That is the amount of time you can save.

Vegetable Stock

Even if you're cooking a vegetarian dish, it's important to start with vegetable stock rather than adding more vegetables to the dish. It creates the background for all other flavors.

Makes 2 quarts | Prep time: 10 minutes | Minimum cook time: 3 hours in a medium slow cooker

2 quarts boiling water

2 carrots, thinly sliced

2 celery ribs, sliced

2 leeks, white parts only, thinly sliced

1 small onion, thinly sliced

1 tablespoon black peppercorns

3 parsley sprigs, rinsed

3 thyme sprigs, rinsed, or 1 teaspoon dried

2 garlic cloves, peeled

1 bay leaf

1. Pour water into the slow cooker, and add carrots, celery, leeks, onion, peppercorns, parsley, thyme, garlic, and bay leaf. Cook on Low for 6 to 8 hours or on High for 3 to 4 hours, or until vegetables are soft.

2. Strain stock through a sieve into a mixing bowl. Press down on solids with the back of a spoon to extract as much liquid as possible. Discard solids.

3. Chill stock, and then ladle stock into containers.

Note: The stock can be refrigerated for up to 4 days, or frozen for up to 6 months.

> Save the water you use when boiling mildly flavored vegetables such as carrots or green beans, and make them part of the liquid used for the stock. However, the water from any member of the cabbage family, like broccoli or cauliflower, is too strong.

Seafood Stock

Seafood stock is delicious in recipes. If you have a fishmonger nearby who sells cooked lobster meat, they'll either give you the shells or charge you a very modest amount for them.

Makes 2 quarts | Prep time: 10 minutes | Minimum cook time: 4 hours in a medium slow cooker

3 lobster bodies (whole lobsters from which the tail and claw meat has been removed) or 2 lobster bodies and the shells from 2 pounds raw shrimp

2½ quarts boiling water

1 carrot, cut into ½-inch chunks

2 leeks, white parts only, sliced

1 celery rib, sliced

1 tablespoon black peppercorns

3 parsley sprigs, rinsed

3 thyme sprigs, rinsed, or 1 teaspoon dried

3 sprigs fresh tarragon, or 1 teaspoon dried

2 garlic cloves, peeled

1 bay leaf

1. Pull the top shell off the lobster body. Scrape off and discard feathery gills, then break the body into small pieces. Place pieces into the slow cooker, and repeat with remaining lobster bodies. Add shrimp shells, if used.

2. Pour boiling water into the slow cooker, and add carrots, leeks, celery, peppercorns, parsley, thyme, tarragon, garlic, and bay leaf. Cook on Low for 8 to 10 hours or on High for 4 to 5 hours, or until vegetables are soft.

3. Strain stock through a sieve into a mixing bowl. Press down on solids with the back of a spoon to extract as much liquid as possible. Discard solids.

4. Chill stock, and then ladle stock into containers.

Note: The stock can be refrigerated for up to 4 days, or frozen for up to 6 months.

Variation:
* Substitute 1½ pounds fish trimmings such as skin, bones, and heads from any firm-fleshed white fish such as snapper or cod for the shellfish for Fish Stock.

Although there are now a lot of commercial fish and seafood stocks on the market, in a pinch you can also substitute diluted bottled clam juice. Use a proportion of two-thirds clam juice to one-third water.

Chapter 2

Low-Acid Breakfasts

The classic American breakfast may consist of orange juice, eggs, toast, and bacon, sausage, or ham, but a reflux-free breakfast should avoid citrus and high-fat, processed meats. Those breakfast meats aren't healthy anyway. As alternatives, this chapter has some wonderfully delicious—and very simple to prepare—recipes that will keep breakfast interesting. Preparing them in the slow cooker allows you to have hot, healthy breakfasts ready for you when you wake up, making it even easier to eat well.

Orange juice is something you may just have to learn to live without. But if you can't bear to give up coffee or tea, limit yourself to a single cup a day, and go ahead and indulge.

Oatmeal for a Crowd

When the whole family is visiting and you want to wake up to a hot, healthy breakfast, use this crowd-pleasing recipe. Don't forget the toppings!

Makes 8 servings.

8 cups water

2 cups steel-cut oats (do not substitute rolled oats or quick-cooking oats)

¼ teaspoon salt, or to taste

Optional toppings: maple syrup, brown sugar, milk, bananas, blueberries, mango, raspberries, Red Delicious apples

1. Combine water, oats, and salt in a 5- or 6-quart slow cooker. Turn heat to Low. Put the lid on and cook until the oats are tender and the porridge is creamy, 7 to 8 hours.

2. Before serving, sweeten with a moderate amount of brown sugar or maple syrup, and if you like to add milk or cream, use products that are fat-free or very low in fat.

Steel-cut oats are different from the rolled oats typically used to make oatmeal. Rather than a flattened kernel (that has sometimes also been pre-cooked, as for instant oatmeal), steel-cut oats are the inner portion of the oat kernel, cut into two or three pieces by steel blades. Thus the name *steel-cut oats*. They take longer to cook and yield a thick, rich porridge. They are perfect for the slow cooker!

Oatmeal with Pumpkin

Pumpkin is both delicious and nutritious. This is a great way to enjoy it for breakfast.

Makes 6 servings.

6 cups water

1 15-oz can pumpkin puree

1½ cups steel-cut oats

½ cup brown sugar

2 tablespoons ground cinnamon

1 tablespoon pumpkin pie spice (or dashes of ginger, nutmeg, and clove to taste)

1. Spray inside of slow cooker with non-stick cooking spray to coat the bottom and sides.

2. Stir water, pumpkin puree, oats, brown sugar, cinnamon, and other spices together. Pour mixture into the prepared slow cooker.

3. Cook on Low for 6 hours. Stir before serving.

You can buy a jar of pumpkin pie spice that contains ginger, nutmeg, and clove. This pre-formulated combo is easy to use and, if you like all these spices, gives you all the flavors you're looking for in one convenient package. If you don't like one of these, or if you want to add more of something, you can buy the spices individually. It's fun to experiment with them, too.

Banana Oatmeal

There's something about bananas that makes hot cereals especially tasty. Slow cooking them with the oatmeal intensifies the flavors.

Makes 6 servings.

5 cups water

1 cup steel-cut oats

2 tablespoons brown sugar

3 ripe bananas, peeled and mashed

Sliced bananas for topping

1. Spray inside of slow cooker with non-stick cooking spray to coat the bottom and sides.

2. Stir water, oats, brown sugar, and mashed bananas together, then pour into the prepared slow cooker. Cook on Low for 6 hours.

3. Stir before serving, and top with sliced bananas.

When the bananas are cooked in with the oatmeal, they soften and blend in with the oats, making for that intense banana flavor that's sometimes found in hand-made banana ice cream or banana bread that has really ripe bananas in it. So tasty!

Oatmeal-Stuffed Pears

Instead of making a cereal that has pears added, try this fun presentation of pears that have been stuffed with the oatmeal. Festive—and delicious!

Makes 4 servings.

3 to 4 ripe Bosc pears

1 cup steel cut oats

¼ cup brown sugar

½ cup butter (softened)

½ teaspoon nutmeg

1¼ teaspoons cinnamon

2 cups apple juice

2 cups water

1. Leaving the peel on, cut pears in half and core.

2. In a small bowl, combine the oats, sugar, butter, nutmeg, and cinnamon. Stir until the mixture is crumbly.

3. Arrange the pears in the slow cooker, peel side down. Place spoonfuls of the oat mixture on top of the pears as if you were stuffing them. Layer the stuffed pears if necessary.

4. Sprinkle any excess oat mixture over all the pears, and then pour the apple juice and water over everything. Cook on Low overnight for 6 to 8 hours.

Finding a ripe pear is such a treat! It seems like they're either over-ripe or under-ripe. An advantage of filling them with oatmeal and then cooking them in the slow cooker is that you can use pears that are on the under-ripe side. They'll soften when they cook, but they'll retain some firmness, which gives great texture to the dish when it's ready.

Multi-Grain Hot Breakfast Cereal

A rib-sticking breakfast full of delicious grains with fruit and spices for added sweetness.

Makes 6 servings.

2½ tablespoons buckwheat groats

2½ tablespoons brown rice

4 tablespoons quinoa

¼ cup rolled oats

1 cup Fuji apple, diced (with peel)

1½ teaspoons ground cinnamon

3 cups water

1 tablespoon vanilla

Optional toppings: bananas, raspberries, apple, low-fat yogurt

1. In a large bowl, combine all ingredients well. Pour into slow cooker. Cover and cook on Low for 6 to 8 hours or overnight. Add more water if desired.

2. For an extra treat, top with sliced bananas, raspberries, or additional apple, and add a spoonful of low-fat yogurt.

This is such a full-bodied, nutty, delicious breakfast treat! Topping the cooked cereal with fruit is wonderful, and for an additional healthy, low-acid treat, consider a spoonful of low-fat Greek or regular yogurt with it, too. If you feel it needs a touch of sweetness, drizzle with just a hint of all-natural maple syrup. Refrain from processed and artificial sugars.

Egg Casserole with Potatoes & Mushrooms

This dish will feed a crowd—or you for a couple of days, which isn't such a bad thing!

Makes 10 to 12 servings.

1 white onion, chopped fine

1 cup sliced domestic mushrooms

2 tablespoons olive oil

4 large Idaho or Yukon Gold potatoes, peeled, washed, and cut into thin slices

1½ cups shredded low-fat Cheddar cheese

12 eggs

1 cup low-fat milk

½ teaspoon salt

1 tablespoon chopped parsley (as garnish)

1. Spray inside of slow cooker with non-stick cooking spray.

2. In small skillet, cook onion and mushrooms in olive oil until tender.

3. Place one-third of the sliced potatoes in the slow cooker. Sprinkle with approximately one-third of the cooked onion/mushroom mix, and then about one-third of the grated cheese. Repeat layers, ending with the cheese.

4. In a large bowl, beat the eggs, milk, and salt until well mixed. Pour over the ingredients in the slow cooker. Cook on Low for 8 to 10 hours, until casserole is set and eggs are thoroughly cooked. If you want to cook on High, it should take 3 to 5 hours depending on how hot your slow cooker gets. To test for doneness, insert a clean knife in the center. If it comes out clean, the eggs are set and potatoes are cooked. Garnish with chopped parsley.

This recipe uses a dozen eggs and makes a satisfying breakfast for a large group. Because of its long cooking time on Low, it is a great meal to put together before you go to bed so that you can wake up to its gooey goodness. Don't forget to garnish with parsley, which adds color, texture, flavor, and vitamins (most notably Vitamin A, which is great for your vision).

Egg, Cheese, and Sausage Casserole

Makes 8 servings.

14 slices whole grain, soft sandwich bread

½ pound turkey sausage, browned and drained twice to remove as much fat as possible

2½ cups grated low-fat cheddar cheese

12 eggs

2¼ cups low-fat milk

1 teaspoon salt

1. Spray inside of slow cooker with non-stick cooking spray.

2. Break up or cut bread into large squares. Layer bread, sausage, and cheese until ingredients are used up.

3. Beat eggs, milk, and salt together. Pour egg mixture into crockpot. Cover and cook on Low for 8 to 12 hours.

A low-acid diet necessitates the limiting of fatty foods, and sausage is certainly one of those. Of course, it is also a great-tasting and satisfying addition to a traditional breakfast. You can satisfy the meat eaters among your friends and family and still be good to yourself if you choose a turkey sausage and brown and drain it twice to remove as much fat as possible. You'll be left with concentrated sausage bites, which, when slow-cooked with the other ingredients, will soften and impart a lot of flavor without the fat.

Broccoli Frittata

This makes a colorful as well as nutritious baked egg dish.

Makes 6 servings.

2 tablespoons olive oil

1 medium white onion, chopped

2 cloves garlic, minced

½ red bell pepper, seeds and ribs removed, thinly sliced

8 large eggs

3 tablespoons low-fat milk

¾ cup fresh broccoli florets, cut into bite-sized pieces

¼ cup Parmesan cheese

2 tablespoons fresh chopped parsley

1 tablespoon fresh thyme

Salt to taste

Non-stick cooking spray

1. Heat the olive oil in a skillet and add onion, garlic, and red pepper. Cook over medium-high heat until onion is translucent, about 3 minutes.

2. In a large bowl, whisk eggs with milk and add broccoli pieces, Parmesan, parsley, and thyme. Add the cooked vegetables.

3. Spray the inside of the slow cooker liberally. Take a large piece of heavy duty aluminum foil, fold it in half, and place it in the slow cooker so the sides come up the sides of the cooker. Pour the egg mixture in on top of the foil.

4. Cover and cook on High for 2 to 2½ hours or until eggs are set.

5. Run a spatula along the sides of the cooker to loosen the foil. Lift the frittata out of the cooker with the foil, and slide it onto a serving plate.

You can substitute frozen broccoli florets for fresh in this recipe. Be sure they are thawed and drained as thoroughly as possible. The cooking time will be the same. If you want to slow-cook this on Low, allow 6 to 8 hours.

Cinnamon Bread Pudding

This is a yummy, gooey, indulgent breakfast dish that can be a treat you make for yourself for a special occasion or a holiday.

Makes 4 servings.

10 slices cinnamon-raisin bread, cut into pieces, about 5 cups

1 (14-oz) can low-fat or fat-free sweetened condensed milk

1 cup water

1 teaspoon vanilla extract

4 eggs, beaten

Non-stick cooking spray

1. Spray the inside of the slow cooker with non-stick cooking spray. Place bread cubes inside.

2. Mix sweetened condensed milk, water, vanilla, and eggs, and pour over the chunks of bread, gently stirring with a wooden spoon to coat the bread with the milk mixture. Cook on Low for 2½ to 3 hours.

3. Serve warm with a spoonful of low-fat yogurt, or with a diced Red Delicious apple.

This is definitely a breakfast for those with a sweet tooth! If you want to reduce the sweetness, you can substitute a thick bread like Challa or a thick-cut white bread for the cinnamon raisin bread. Add ¼ to ½ of a teaspoon of cinnamon to the milk mixture. You can also add a half-cup of dried currants for added flavor and texture.

Whole-Grain Bread

Nothing beats fresh-baked bread for breakfast! Here's a way to do it in your slow cooker. Once you get the hang of it, you can make this to accompany any of your meals.

2½ cups whole wheat flour

1¼ cups white flour

2 cups warm low-fat milk

2 tablespoons vegetable oil

¼ cup honey

¾ teaspoon salt

1 package yeast

Rolled oats for topping

Non-stick cooking spray

1 teaspoon soft butter for greasing the foil

1. Find a bread pan that will fit into your slow cooker, and set it aside while you prepare the dough.

2. In a medium-sized bowl, combine the whole wheat and white flours. In a large bowl, stir together the milk, oil, honey, salt, and yeast. Add 2 cups of the flour mixture. Beat with an electric mixer on Low for two minutes until thoroughly blended. Add the remaining flour and mix well with a large wooden spoon. The dough should be thick and elastic.

3. Spray the bread pan thoroughly with non-stick cooking spray. Transfer the dough into the bread pan. Sprinkle the top with rolled oats. Cover with tin foil that's been greased with butter. Let stand for 5 minutes.

4. Put the bread pan into the slow cooker, cover, and cook on High 2½ to 3 hours. When you remove the pan from the cooker, tap on the bottom. It should sound hollow. Remove the pan, take the foil off the top, and let the bread stand for 5 minutes. Serve warm.

It's so fun to cook bread in the slow cooker! An added bonus is that you can do this in the summer and you don't have to worry about heating up your whole kitchen by turning on the oven. If you want a crispier top to your loaf, you can always finish the bread in the oven, baking it at 350 degrees for 15 to 20 minutes.

Banana Bread

Sure you can make banana bread in the oven, but it's equally successful in the slow cooker. Have fun with this one!

Makes 6 servings.

5 eggs, beaten

3½ cups low-fat milk

2 teaspoons vanilla

2 tablespoons ground cinnamon

½ teaspoon salt

6 cups plain breadcrumbs (or more to make mixture as thick as cooked oatmeal when mixed with all ingredients)

¾ cup packed brown sugar

1 tablespoon butter or 1 tablespoon margarine, melted

2 ripe bananas, mashed or sliced

Non-stick cooking spray

1. In a large bowl, mix all ingredients together until bread crumbs are thoroughly wet, and mixture is smooth like thick oatmeal.

2. Spray the slow cooker with non-stick cooking spray, and transfer the mixture to the slow cooker.

3. Cover and cook on High for 4 to 5 hours—but, for the last half-hour of cooking, open the lid on one side and put the handle of a spoon under to keep the lid propped open. This will allow the moisture to escape. If you don't do this, you will have a layer of liquid all around the bread.

4. When cooked, a knife stuck in the middle will come out fairly clean. Serve warm.

Because the dough for this bread is going in the slow cooker and not in a loaf pan, it'll come out in a circle or oval, depending on the shape of your cooker. It'll still taste amazing. If you want an added taste treat, add a diced pear to the dough before cooking.

Fabulous & Fruity French Toast

Top the slow-cooked French toast with a mixture of berries for flavor and color.

Makes 6 servings.

12 slices whole wheat bread

6 eggs

1 teaspoon vanilla

1 teaspoon lemon zest

2 cups fat-free evaporated milk

2 tablespoons dark brown sugar

1 teaspoon cinnamon

¼ teaspoon nutmeg

2 cups diced fresh fruit, including blackberries, raspberries, and blueberries

Non-stick cooking spray

1. Spray the inside of the slow cooker with non-stick spray. Layer the bread in the slow cooker.

2. In a small bowl, whisk the eggs, vanilla, zest, evaporated milk, brown sugar, cinnamon, and nutmeg. Pour over the bread. Cover and cook on Low for 6 to 8 hours. Then, remove the lid, and cook uncovered for an additional 30 minutes or until the liquid has evaporated somewhat.

3. Divide up the bread and sauce, and garnish with fresh fruit.

This is another great breakfast to wake up to when you make it the night before. In the summertime, it's a warm treat with lots of fresh fruit that hasn't heated up your kitchen or left that just-cooked smell of fried eggs. And it's a great way to use bread that's on the verge of getting stale.

Chapter 3

Soups That Don't Simmer Your Insides

*O*nce you start making soup in your slow cooker, you may never go back to your pot on the stovetop. Slow cooking melds and enhances so many flavors. While your choice of ingredients for the low-acid diet may be limited, it doesn't mean your flavor combinations have to be boring. This chapter is full of recipes that will inspire and delight your senses and that make for very satisfying meals when served with a favorite kind of bread. Enjoy—and experiment!

Super-Simple Split Pea

Rich, green goodness from a simple selection of ingredients is what this soup is all about.

Makes 6 servings.

1 bag green split peas

1 Idaho potato, peeled and cubed

3 to 4 carrots, peeled and cut into slices

1 celery stalk, cleaned and diced, or ½ teaspoon. celery seed

8 cups of water

Salt to taste

1. To prepare, put dried peas into a colander and pick through them to remove any overly dark or dirty ones. Rinse with cold water and shake dry.

2. Add peas and other ingredients into the slow cooker, and cover with water. Cook on Low for 8 hours.

An all-vegetable pea soup is a bowlful of goodness. If you're someone who loves the addition of something smoky and salty in their pea soup, indulge with this recipe. Take three or four slices of thinly sliced prosciutto, cut off and discard the fat, dice the meat, and add it to the other ingredients before putting everything into the slow cooker.

Potage Saint-Germain

This is a lighter version of the classic split pea soup, which tends to be almost stew-like.

2 tablespoons unsalted butter

2 medium white onions, chopped

1 carrot, chopped

2 celery ribs, chopped

2 cups green split peas, rinsed

1 cup frozen peas, thawed

1 cup shredded Romaine lettuce

2 tablespoons chopped fresh parsley

2 tablespoons chopped fresh sage
or 2 teaspoons dried sage

1 tablespoons fresh thyme
or ½ teaspoon dried thyme

1 bay leaf

7 cups low-fat chicken broth

1 cup low-fat milk (optional)

Salt to taste

1. Heat the butter in a skillet. Add chopped onion, carrot, and celery, and cook over medium-high heat until the onion is translucent, about 3 minutes. Put mixture into the slow cooker.

2. Add dried peas, thawed peas, lettuce, parsley, sage, thyme, and bay leaf to the slow cooker and cover with the chicken broth. Stir well. Cover and cook on Low for 6 to 8 hours or on High for 3 to 4 hours, or until split peas have disintegrated.

3. If you've cooked the soup on Low, about one-half hour before serving, turn it to High so the soup is bubbling. Turn off the cooker and take out the bay leaf. Let cool for about 10 minutes.

4. Puree the soup with an immersion blender or do the solids in batches in a food processor or blender.

5. If you'll be serving the soup immediately, add the milk, stir and serve. If you'll be serving the soup later, either transfer the soup to a container and reheat when ready, or keep it on Low in the slow cooker.

With almost all fresh herbs, the substitution with the dried form is 1 tablespoon fresh to 1 teaspoon dried. One exception to this, however, is thyme. The leaves are so small once dried that I've found that ½ teaspoon dried produces the same flavor as 1 tablespoon fresh.

Chickpea Soup with Hearty Greens

The chickpeas are the stars in this satisfying soup full of vitamins.

Makes 8 servings.

1 lb dried chickpeas

1 cup water

6 cups low-fat chicken broth

1 large white onion, chopped

3 garlic cloves, minced

2 bay leaves

1 large head escarole or kale or Swiss chard, chopped, washed, and dried

Salt to taste

Non-stick cooking spray

1. Soak the chickpeas overnight in enough fresh water to cover them. Drain and rinse.

2. Spray the inside of the slow cooker, and put the beans in. Add the water, chicken broth, onion, garlic, and bay leaves. Cover and cook on High for 2 to 3 hours or until beans are tender.

3. When the beans are thoroughly cooked, add the chopped greens. Stir and recover, cooking another 20 to 30 minutes on Low. Stir and serve.

The chickpea is an ancient legume originating in the Middle East, where it was cultivated about 3000 BC. A staple of Roman, Greek, and Egyptian diets for centuries, it only made its way to Spain in the 16th century. Today it is enjoyed the world over for its nutty yet buttery flavor and its high protein and fiber, making it an excellent substitute for meat. It's called the *garbanzo bean* in Spanish cooking, and the *ceci* in Italian.

Cabbage and Carrot Soup

You'll find the carrots mellow the cabbage in this soup with a beautiful flavor and texture.

Makes 4 servings.

4 tablespoons unsalted butter

1 tablespoon vegetable oil

1 large white onion, chopped

1 lb green cabbage, sliced thin and washed

2 small zucchini, washed and sliced thin

2 carrots, peeled and sliced thin

1 Fuji apple, peeled and sliced thin

4 cups low-fat chicken broth

Salt to taste

Non-stick cooking spray

1. Heat the butter and oil in a skillet and add the onion. Cook over medium-high heat until onions are translucent, about 3 minutes.

2. Spray the inside of the slow cooker with non-stick cooking spray and add the cabbage, zucchini, carrots, apple, and cooked onion.

3. Add the chicken broth, cover, and cook on High for 2 hours. Check the soup. The cabbage should be cooked but still fairly firm. Turn to Low and cook for another 20 to 30 minutes until heated through. Season to taste with salt and serve.

When cooking bulky foods such as cabbage, chances are good that all the cabbage will not be covered with broth at the beginning of the cooking process. About midway through, it will have wilted considerably and you can push it down.

Puréed Zucchini Soup with Curry

Zucchini is such a versatile vegetable that it's no wonder it makes a great soup, too. The addition of curry takes the taste up a notch. You could substitute dill or thyme, too.

Makes 4 to 6 servings.

1 tablespoon olive oil

1 small white onion, chopped

2 garlic cloves, minced

2 lbs zucchini, diced (about 7 cups diced)

2 teaspoon curry powder

6 cups low-fat chicken stock

¼ cup basmati rice

Salt to taste

Croutons for garnish (optional)

1. Heat the olive oil over medium heat in skillet and add the onion. Cook, stirring, until it is tender, about 5 minutes.

2. Into the slow cooker, put the garlic, zucchini, cooked onions, a generous pinch of salt, and the curry powder. Stir well to combine. Add the stock and rice, and stir again to mix. Cover and cook on Low 5 to 7 hours or on High 2 to 3 hours. Season to taste with salt.

3. Purée the soup with an immersion blender or in batches in a food processor or blender. Serve with croutons.

Zucchini is Italian in origin, and its native name was retained when it was integrated into American cooking. Choose small zucchini because they tend to have a sweeter flavor and the seeds are tender and less pronounced.

Jerusalem Artichoke Soup

A Jerusalem artichoke looks like a strange form of potato—and it is indeed a tuber vegetable—which makes it a great root vegetable to use as a base for a rich soup. It has the flavor of an artichoke or water chestnut, though, and the combination with pears brings out a slight sweetness.

Makes 6 to 8 servings.

8 tablespoons butter

3 lbs Jerusalem artichokes, peeled and sliced

2 white onions, sliced

3 Bosc pears, peeled, cored, and diced

4 cups water

4 cups low-fat milk

Pinch of sugar

Salt to taste

Non-stick cooking spray

1. In a large saucepan, heat the butter and add the Jerusalem artichokes and onions. Cook over medium-high heat for about 10 minutes until the onion is soft.

2. Spray the inside of the slow cooker with non-stick cooking spray. Add the pears, artichoke-and-onion mixture, and water. Cover and cook on High 2 to 3 hours or until cooked through and soft.

3. Puree the soup with an immersion blender or puree in batches in a food processor or blender.

4. Add the milk, and season with salt and a pinch of sugar.

Another name for the Jerusalem artichoke is the sunchoke. The tuber is native to North America, where settlers learned of it in Virginia in the 1500s. When the tuber was brought to Europe, they became very popular, as they were easy to grow in many areas. It is believed they got their misleading name from a variation of the Italian word for them, *girasola*, which translates to "turning toward the sun," which is what their tall flowers do in the garden.

Vegetable Soup with Herb Oil

What makes this soup so special is the contrast between the mellow, long-simmered flavors of the soup and the freshness of the herb oil.

Makes 4 to 6 servings.

SOUP

3 tablespoons olive oil

1 medium white onion, diced

1 clove garlic, minced

2 large carrots, peeled and sliced

½ fennel bulb, cored and sliced

2 cups firmly packed, thinly sliced green cabbage

5 cups vegetable stock

2 tablespoons chopped fresh parsley

1 teaspoon dried oregano

1 tablespoon fresh thyme

1 bay leaf

1 medium zucchini, diced

1 medium yellow squash, diced

1 15-oz can garbanzo beans, drained and rinsed

Parmesan cheese (optional)

¼ lb whole-grain pasta shells, cooked according to package until al dente

Salt to taste

HERB OIL

¾ cup firmly packed parsley leaves

1 clove garlic, minced

2 tablespoons chopped fresh basil

1 tablespoon chopped fresh rosemary

½ cup olive oil

Salt to taste

1. Heat oil in a large skillet over medium-high heat. Add onion, garlic, carrot, fennel, and cabbage. Cook, stirring frequently, for about 3 minutes, or until onion is translucent. Scrape mixture into the slow cooker.

2. Add stock, parsley, oregano, thyme, and bay leaf and stir all ingredients together. Cook on Low for 4 to 6 hours or on High for 2 to 3 hours, or until vegetables are tender.

3. Add zucchini and yellow squash, and cook on Low for an additional 2 hours, or on High for 1 additional hour, until these are tender, too.

4. If cooking on Low, turn heat to High. Add beans to the slow cooker and cook for another 15 to 20 minutes, or until simmering.

5. Remove and discard bay leaf, add cooked pasta, and season with salt.

6. While soup simmers, prepare herb oil by combining parsley, garlic, basil, rosemary, and olive oil in a food processor or blender. Puree until smooth, season with salt, and scrape mixture into a bowl.

7. Ladle soup into bowls to serve, passing the herb oil and Parmesan cheese (if desired).

> When soups are made with pasta, the cooked pasta should be added just prior to serving. Otherwise it will absorb stock from the soup and get mushy.

Sugar Pea Pod Soup

This vibrantly green soup is brightened in flavor by the sweetness of the sugar peas.

Makes 8 servings.

4 tablespoons butter

1 cup thinly sliced leeks (white parts only)

3 tablespoons flour

1 teaspoon salt

10-oz package frozen peas

1 lb fresh snow peas or sugar snap peas, strings removed

8 large leaves Boston lettuce

4 cups low-fat chicken broth

1½ cups water

1 cup low-fat milk (optional)

Salt to taste

Non-stick cooking spray

1. Heat the butter in a skillet and add the leeks, cooking over medium-high heat until translucent, about 3 to 5 minutes. Sprinkle the flour over the leeks and butter, and stir together.

2. Spray the slow cooker with non-stick cooking spray. Add the frozen peas, snow peas, and lettuce leaves. Put the leek mixture in, then cover with the chicken broth, stirring to coat everything. Add the water. Cover and cook on High for 1½ to 2 hours or until peas are cooked through and soft.

3. Puree with an immersion blender or in batches in a food processor or blender. You can set aside and serve as a cold soup, or serve immediately as a hot soup. You can also make it a creamier soup by adding the milk. Garnish with additional Boston lettuce leaves if desired.

It's important to clean leeks thoroughly, as they are typically grown in sandy soil and often retain that grittiness. To do so, place the sliced leeks for the recipe in a bowl of clean, cold water in which the water completely covers the leeks. Swirl and splash them around to loosen the sand or dirt. Scoop out the leeks and put the slices in a colander. Give a final rinse in the colander, shake off excess water, and you're good to go.

Sweet Potato and Apple Soup

A fall vegetable and a fall fruit together make a delicious, warming soup.

Makes 10 servings.

1 tablespoon butter

1 large white onion, chopped

2 lbs sweet potatoes, peeled and cubed

½ lb carrots, peeled and cubed

2 Gala or Fuji apples,
peeled, cored, and cubed

3 cups low-fat chicken broth

1 cup water

Fresh thyme for garnish

Non-stick cooking spray

1. Heat the butter in a skillet and add the onion, cooking over medium-high heat until translucent, about 3 to 5 minutes.

2. Spray the slow cooker, add the sweet potatoes, carrots, and apples, then stir in the cooked onions. Add the chicken broth and water, stir again, cover and cook on High for 2 to 2½ hours until veggies are soft and cooked through.

3. Puree with an immersion blender or in batches in a food processor or blender. Serve hot and garnish with a sprig of thyme if desired.

Not only is this soup delicious, it is packed with the nutrients of its key ingredient: sweet potatoes. To get the most from the healthy supply of carbohydrates, fiber, protein, and vitamins A, B6, and C that they're known for, choose sweet potatoes with darker flesh, and use ones that are as fresh and locally grown as possible.

Chicken Soup with Fennel and Escarole

This easy-to-make chicken soup has a delicious hint of licorice from the fresh fennel.

Makes 6 to 8 servings.

1 lb boneless, skinless chicken from thighs or breasts

1 large fennel bulb, cored and cut into squares

3 tablespoons olive oil

1 large white onion, diced

2 cloves garlic, minced

2 teaspoons fennel seeds, crushed

5 cups low-fat chicken broth

1 head escarole

Salt to taste

1. Rinse chicken and pat dry with paper towels. Trim chicken of all visible fat, and cut into ½-inch cubes. Place chicken and fennel in the slow cooker.

2. Heat olive oil in a medium skillet over medium-high heat. Add onions and garlic and cook, stirring frequently, for about 3 minutes or until onion is translucent.

3. Put the onion mixture into the slow cooker, then the fennel seeds, then the broth. Stir to combine.

4. Cook on Low for 5 to 7 hours or on High for 2 to 3 hours, or until chicken is cooked through and no longer pink.

5. While soup cooks, rinse escarole and discard core. Slice escarole into 1-inch wide strips.

6. Add the escarole to the slow cooker and cook for an additional 30 minutes until escarole is wilted. If cooking on Low, raise heat to High. Season with salt and serve hot.

Fresh fennel, *finocchio* in Italian, and sometimes called *anise* in supermarkets, has a slightly licorice taste but the texture of celery—both raw and cooked. You can always substitute 2 celery ribs for each ½ fennel bulb specified in a recipe.

Pumpkin & Pear Soup

Another soup made from classic fall foods that is a winner any time you make it.

Makes 6 servings.

2 tablespoons butter

1 large white onion, chopped

2 lbs pumpkin (or butternut squash) peeled, seeded, and cut into 2-inch pieces

2 Bosc pears, peeled, cored and cubed

4 carrots, peeled and cut into thin slices

6 cups low-fat chicken broth

Sprigs of fresh thyme

6 fresh sage leaves

Salt to taste

Non-stick cooking spray

1. Heat the butter in a skillet and add the onions, cooking over medium-high heat until translucent, about 3 to 5 minutes.

2. Spray the inside of the slow cooker, and add the pumpkin, pears, and carrots. Stir in the chicken broth. Add the cooked onions and stir. Put three thyme sprigs on top. Cover and cook on High 2 to 3 hours or until vegetables and fruit are cooked through and soft.

3. Remove the thyme sprigs. Puree with an immersion blender or in batches in a food processor or blender. Season to taste with salt. Serve hot. Garnish with the sage leaves and some additional thyme if desired.

You can substitute canned pumpkin puree for fresh pumpkin or butternut squash. The ratio is 1:1. In this recipe, if the 2 pounds of pumpkin peeled and diced yields about 2 cups, you can substitute 16 ounces of canned pumpkin puree. The flavor difference will be minimal.

Rice Soup

This is a take on the ancient Asian soup, or porridge, called *congee*. It is essentially rice cooked slowly until it forms a thick soup. This recipe flavors the soup with ginger and cilantro, but in Asian cuisines the variations are many and can include spices, vegetables, and meats or fish as well as herbs.

Makes 10 servings.

1½ cups uncooked white or jasmine rice

15 cups water

¼ cup minced fresh ginger

3 scallions, white part only, chopped fine

1½ tablespoons coarse salt

1¼ cups cilantro, washed, dried, and chopped

Non-stick cooking spray

1. Spray the slow cooker with the cooking spray. Add the rice, cover with the water, stir, cover, and cook on High for 2 to 3 hours. The rice should be completely cooked through, soft and soupy.

2. Stir in the ginger, scallions, salt, and 1 cup of the cilantro. Cover but turn off the slow cooker. Let sit for 20 to 30 minutes. Stir and serve hot, garnishing with additional cilantro.

If you have an especially busy week coming up, you can double the recipe for this rice soup. That way you'll have it on hand when you get home and want a quick, filling, hot meal. You can add almost anything to it to dress it up—make it spices one night, steamed veggies another, or mix and match with what you have in the pantry.

Bean, Corn, and Barley Soup

Barley is an ancient grain that is used in Italy's northern provinces. It creates a thick and robust soup flavored with many vegetables and herbs, as well as cannellini beans.

1 tablespoon olive oil

1 medium white onion, minced

2 cloves garlic, minced

1 celery rib, washed and the fronds removed, sliced thin

¾ pearl barley, rinsed well

5 cups low-fat chicken broth

¼ cup fresh parsley, chopped

1 tablespoon fresh rosemary, chopped

1 bay leaf

1 15-oz can cannellini beans, drained and rinsed

¾ cup fresh corn kernels, or frozen kernels, thawed

Salt to taste

Parmesan cheese (optional)

1. Heat oil in a large skillet over medium-high heat. Add onion, garlic, and celery and cook, stirring, for about 3 minutes or until onion is translucent. Scrape mixture into the slow cooker.

2. Add the barley, broth, parsley, rosemary, and bay leaf to the slow cooker and stir well to combine. Cook on Low for 6 to 8 hours or on High for 3 to 4 hours, until vegetables are tender.

3. If cooking on Low, raise heat to High. Stir in the beans and corn, and cook for an additional 30 to 40 minutes, until vegetables are heated through.

4. Remove and discard bay leaf, and season with salt to taste.

5. Serve hot, topping with Parmesan if desired.

Barley is an ancient grain favored by Italians when making thick and robust soups. If the flavor isn't for you, though, you can substitute buckwheat or quinoa. Both will cook in the same amount of time as the barley. The soup will not be as thick, however, if you substitute with those grains.

Watercress Soup

If you like the tangy yet delicate flavor of watercress, you will love this soup, which is thickened with tofu.

Makes 10 servings.

1 cup washed and shredded cabbage leaves

2 bunches watercress, washed, dried, and some stalk removed

2 large Portobello mushrooms, washed, patted dry, and chopped

8 cups low-fat chicken broth

4 cups water

4 tablespoons cornstarch, dissolved in 4 tablespoons water (rice flour or arrowroot may be used as a substitute for the cornstarch)

2 scallions, white part only, sliced thin

1 cup tofu, cubed

Non-stick cooking spray

1. Spray the slow cooker. Add the cabbage, watercress, mushrooms, broth, and water. Cover and cook on High for 1½ to 2 hours.

2. When liquid is bubbly and cooked through, stir in the cornstarch and continue stirring with slow cooker on High for a minute or so until thoroughly blended. Stir in the scallions and tofu and serve hot.

Arrowroot is an excellent substitute for cornstarch when you want to thicken a recipe. It is a powder made from the tropical arrowroot plant. It can be more difficult to find in the grocery store, but it is healthier overall than cornstarch, as it is easier to digest. It imparts no flavor, either.

Chinese Pork Soup with Rice Noodles

Soups make wonderful main dishes, especially when loaded with vegetables that remain fairly crunchy, even after cooking, and infused with toasted sesame oil.

Makes 4 to 6 servings.

1 lb boneless pork loin

3 tablespoons low-sodium soy sauce

2 tablespoons Asian sesame oil, divided

1 tablespoon vegetable oil

2 scallions, white part and 4 inches of green tops, sliced

2 garlic cloves, minced

1 tablespoon fresh ginger, grated

4 cups bok choy cabbage, washed and chopped

5 cups low-fat chicken stock

1 teaspoon rice wine vinegar

1 tablespoon brown sugar

5 oz thick rice noodles

3 tablespoons fresh cilantro, chopped

Salt to taste

1. Trim pork of all visible fat, and cut into very thin slices. Place pork in the slow cooker and toss it with the soy sauce and 1 tablespoon of the sesame oil.

2. Heat remaining sesame oil and vegetable oil in a small skillet over medium-high heat. Add scallions, garlic, and ginger. Cook, stirring constantly, for 30 seconds or until fragrant. Scrape mixture into the slow cooker.

3. Add bok choy, broth, vinegar, and sugar to the slow cooker, and stir to combine. Cook on Low for 4 to 6 hours, or on High for 2 to 3 hours, until pork is cooked through.

4. If cooking on Low, raise the heat to High. Add the noodles and cilantro to the soup, and season to taste with salt. Cook for an additional 15 to 20 minutes, or until noodles are soft and soup is bubbly.

Delicate rice noodles cook faster than starchier, wheat-based noodles. In fact, they really only need to soften. If making dishes with rice vermicelli, soaking the noodles in hot tap water for less than 1 minute will do the trick. For thicker noodles, they need no more than a few minutes of simmering.

Asparagus Soup

If you crave a soup that has the flavor association of spring, this dish rich with asparagus is the one for you.

Makes 4 servings.

3 tablespoons butter

1 white onion, chopped

2 lbs asparagus, trimmed and cut into ½-inch pieces

1 teaspoon dried tarragon, crumbled

4 cups chicken broth

½ cup plain low-fat yogurt

Non-stick cooking spray

1. In a skillet, heat the butter, add the onion, and cook over medium-high heat until the onion is translucent, about 3 minutes.

2. Spray the slow cooker. Add the asparagus, onion mix, tarragon, and chicken broth. Cover and cook on High for 1 to 2 hours until asparagus is tender and cooked through.

3. Puree with an immersion blender or in batches in a food processor or blender.

4. Add the yogurt, stir, and serve.

To maximize the taste and nutrient value of asparagus, get them when they're freshest —usually April or May. Look for straight, firm stalks, thick or thin. Asparagus deteriorate rapidly once picked, so use them soon after purchasing. Store them upright in a bowl or vase of cold water, or wrap the ends in a damp towel and refrigerate. Cut off the woody ends before cooking.

Brussels Sprout Soup

A bit mellower than its cousin the cabbage, but still very much a member of the cruciferous vegetable family that also includes kale and cauliflower, Brussels sprouts are loaded with Vitamin C and other cholesterol-fighting nutrients. And they make a tasty soup.

Makes 4 servings.

½ lb chicken sausage, cut into thin slices

1 tablespoon butter

Medium white onion, chopped

20 oz fresh Brussels sprouts, trimmed, or 2 10-oz packages of frozen Brussels sprouts, thawed

3 large carrots, peeled and sliced

4 Yukon Gold potatoes, cut into ½-inch cubes

4 cups low-fat chicken broth

2 cups water

Salt to taste

Non-stick cooking spray

1. In a skillet over medium heat, cook the chicken sausage until lightly browned on all sides. Place on a plate covered with a paper towel to absorb the excess grease. Clean the pan or use a clean one. Heat the butter, add the onion, and cook over medium high heat until the onion is translucent, about 3 minutes.

2. If using fresh Brussels sprouts, coarsely chop them. If using thawed sprouts, cut them in half.

3. Spray the slow cooker with non-stick cooking spray. Add the Brussels sprouts, carrots, potatoes, onion mixture, sausage, broth, and water. Cover and cook on High for 2 to 3 hours. Serve hot.

The chicken sausage in this soup gives it delicious saltiness and texture. To minimize the amount of fat, it's important to cut the sausage into small pieces before sautéing and frequently drain any fat that is produced while cooking. With thorough cooking, and by placing on a paper towel afterward to absorb any excess fat, the sausage is ready to use.

Salmon Chowder

A wonderful soup to serve for a special occasion—or as a substitute for a vacation to the coast!

Makes 4 servings.

1 lb Yukon Gold potatoes, peeled and cubed

1 teaspoon salt

3 cups low-fat milk

2 cups water

4 tablespoons butter

1 cup minced white onion

1 lb salmon steak, skinned and boned

2 tablespoons flour

4 oz smoked salmon, chopped fine (optional)

4 tablespoons fresh dill, chopped,
or 2 teaspoons dried, crumbled

Non-stick cooking spray

1. Spray the slow cooker with non-stick cooking spray. Put in the potatoes, salt, milk, and water. Cover and cook on High for about 2 hours until the potatoes are tender.

2. When potatoes have about a half-hour left to cook, heat the butter in a saucepan, add the onion, and cook until it is softened. Put the salmon on the onion, sprinkle with salt, lower the heat to Low or Medium, and cover with the saucepan lid so that the salmon steak cooks. Turn after about 4 minutes. It should take about 10 minutes to cook through.

3. Transfer the cooked salmon to a plate.

4. Sprinkle the flour over the onion mixture and stir, cooking on medium for about 3 minutes.

5. With a large spoon or ladle, transfer some of the hot milk/water mixture from the slow cooker and stir it into the onion mixture. Do this gradually until the flour is stirred in thoroughly. Put the onion/flour mixture in with the potatoes and liquid, and stir. Cover and cook on Low for about 20 minutes.

6. When ready to serve, add the salmon steak, breaking it into chunks and stirring it into the potato soup. Allow to heat through, and serve.

Although it hasn't been traced with complete accuracy, it is believed that the word *chowder* comes from the French term *faire la chaudiere,* which translates to "make something in a cauldron." It is theorized that fishermen in coastal Brittany brought the term from France to Nova Scotia. The Old English word *jowter,* for fish peddler, is also considered an originator for chowder. Chowders are traditionally associated with seafood; salmon was popularized in the Pacific Northwest.

Oh, So Satisfying Shrimp and Vegetable Soup

This is a fun soup to make. It's a playful combination of vegetables and shrimp, with a nice dollop of dill.

Makes 4 servings.

2 carrots, peeled and sliced thin

1½ cups shelled fresh peas
or frozen peas, thawed

2 cups cauliflower florets, cubed

2 Yukon Gold potatoes, peeled and cubed

½ lb fresh green beans, trimmed and cut into ½-inch pieces

4 cups water

4 oz fresh baby spinach, stems removed, washed, and dried thoroughly

2 large egg yolks

1 cup fat free half-and-half

½ lb small shrimp, shelled and deveined

2 teaspoons salt

2 tablespoons fresh dill, chopped (optional)

Non-stick cooking spray

1. Spray the slow cooker. Add the carrots, peas, cauliflower, potatoes, green beans, and water. Cover and cook on High for 2 hours. Open the slow cooker and add the spinach, reduce heat to Low, and cook another hour.

2. In a small bowl, whisk together the egg yolks and half-and-half. Open the slow cooker and put 1 cup of the vegetable mixture into a measuring cup. Add gradually to the egg/cream mixture. When thoroughly mixed, put this blend into the slow cooker with the rest, and stir to combine. With the broth heated but not boiling, add the shrimp. Cover and cook until the shrimp are pink and just firm.

3. Season to taste with salt, and serve, garnishing with dill if desired.

Dill has an interesting sour flavor that is prized in pickling, as well as in soups like this one. The use of dill dates back to biblical times, and it was even considered an aphrodisiac at one time. This recipe calls for fresh dill. If you are a huge fan, you may want to add a pinch of dill seeds to the soup, too.

Chicken and Corn Soup

For a thicker soup with more texture, include pasta or rice. For a soup that's a lighter but flavorful broth, leave out the pasta or rice.

Makes 6 servings.

2 tablespoons olive oil

2 large ribs celery, finely diced

1 medium onion, finely diced

1 pinch saffron threads

½ teaspoon dried thyme

2 carrots, peeled and cut into thin slices

8 cups chicken broth

2 cups finely diced or shredded cooked chicken

1 cup frozen corn

¼ cup chopped fresh flat-leaf parsley

Optional: 1 cup of cooked pasta or rice

Salt to taste

Non-stick cooking spray

1. Heat the oil in a saucepan over medium heat. Add the celery, onion, saffron, and thyme. Cook, stirring occasionally, until the vegetables start to soften, about 5 minutes.

2. Spray the slow cooker. Put the vegetable mixture in it, and the carrots, and add the broth. Cover and cook on High for 1 to 2 hours. Add the chicken and replace the cover, cooking another 30 to 40 minutes. Add the corn and parsley, and stir until it is warmed through.

3. For a fuller-bodied soup, add a cup or so of cooked pasta or rice. (These should be cooked separately so as not to over-starch the soup while cooking.)

4. Season to taste with salt, and serve.

There is evidence to support the idea that chicken stock really does contain medicinal qualities. In 1993, University of Nebraska Medical Center researcher Dr. Stephen Rennard published a study stating that chicken soup contains an anti-inflammatory mechanism that eases the symptoms of upper respiratory tract infection. Other studies also showed that the chicken soup was equally medicinal if made without vegetables; it was the chicken itself that did the trick.

Bean and Greens Soup

Mix and match the greens you add to this soup for added flavor.

Makes 6 servings.

6 cups vegetable broth

1 15-oz can great northern beans, drained and rinsed

½ cup brown rice, uncooked

½ cup white onion, finely chopped

1 teaspoon dried basil

¼ teaspoon salt

4 garlic cloves, chopped

8 cups fresh spinach, kale, collard, or chard leaves (or a combination of the above), coarsely chopped

Parmesan cheese for garnish

1. In the slow cooker, combine broth, beans, rice, onion, basil, salt, and garlic. Cover and cook on Low for 5 to 7 hours or on High for 2 to 3 hours.

2. Just before serving, stir in greens. Continue cooking for 5 to 10 minutes. Serve hot, garnishing with Parmesan cheese if desired.

Not everyone is familiar with great northern beans. They are similar to navy and cannellini beans. In fact, if you can't find them, you can substitute either of these. The navy beans are a bit smaller, and the cannellini a bit larger. The flavor profiles are similar, with slight variations in nuttiness.

Fennel and Potato Soup

A root vegetable-based soup with hints of licorice. A mainstream variation on this recipe calls for lots of garlic, as well, to further enhance the flavor. If desired, try adding a small amount and, if your system can handle it, increase the number of cloves, but don't add more than six per batch.

Makes 6 servings.

2 tablespoons olive oil

½ large or 1 medium white onion, diced

2 stalks celery, sliced

2 lbs bulb fennel, trimmed, washed and diced

Salt to taste

1 lb Yukon gold potatoes, peeled and diced

2 to 6 garlic cloves, peeled and cut in half

A bouquet garni made with a bay leaf, a couple of sprigs each parsley and thyme, and ½ teaspoon fennel seeds, tied in cheesecloth

2 quarts water, low-fat vegetable stock, or low-fat chicken stock

Chopped fresh fennel fronds for garnish

Non-stick cooking spray

1. Heat the olive oil in a large saucepan over medium heat and add the onion, celery, fennel, and a generous pinch of salt. Cook gently for about 5 to 8 minutes, until the vegetables have softened.

2. Spray the slow cooker with the cooking spray. Add the potatoes, garlic, bouquet garni, cooked vegetable mixture, and the water or stock. Cover and cook 5 to 7 hours on Low or 2 to 3 hours on High.

3. Remove the bouquet garni. Blend the soup until smooth with an immersion blender, or puree in batches in a food processor or blender. Add salt to taste and serve hot, garnishing with the fennel fronds. If desired, transfer to a container, allow to chill, cover, and refrigerate to serve cold.

The bouquet garni is a collection of herbs traditionally used to flavor soups and stews. Parsley, thyme, and bay leaf are the classic combination. When prepared fresh, they are tied together with a kitchen string so that they can be easily removed. In this recipe, fennel seed is added to the combo, and the ingredients are put into a piece of cheesecloth. You can substitute 1 tablespoon dried parsley, 1 teaspoon dried thyme, and 1 dried bay leaf for the fresh herbs. Tie the cheesecloth securely.

Chapter 4

Pasta Sauces:
No Tomatoes Allowed!

When you think of pasta, it's hard not to think of tomatoes. Nearly every spaghetti sauce contains them, and even recipes like stuffed shells or lasagna are hard to imagine without them. But it is possible, and as someone on a low-acid diet, you'll be impressed with how quickly you can get creative with pasta. This chapter includes a variety of meat sauces, chicken sauces, seafood sauces, and vegetable sauces.

The good news is that you can eat almost any kind of pasta. As discussed earlier, if you choose whole grain pastas, you'll be eating even healthier, but regular pastas are fine, too. Like soup or stew, a steaming bowl of pasta with a simple sauce is one of the most delicious and satisfying meals you can have— and you can make it in a crowd-pleasing quantity.

For reflux sufferers, while the slow cooker is a blessing for long-range planning, there are quick, healthy meals you can make without it that can be rotated into the mix and which can be elaborated on in the slow cooker. Get to know which herbs you like, and experiment with combinations of them sprinkled on hot pasta. Buy a steamer bag of frozen vegetables, and by the time you've cooked the pasta, you can add the cooked veggies to your pasta, season lightly, and serve.

Angel Hair Pasta with Fresh Herbs

While not one to make in the slow cooker, this simple recipe is an example of the many ways you can enjoy pasta with different combinations of herbs. Use fresh thyme, rosemary, or sage—or a blend of these. Try dill. Fresh herbs are preferable to dried. If you like anchovies, you're in luck. They give this simple dish an added depth.

Makes 4 to 6 servings.

1 lb angel hair pasta (regular or whole grain)

Extra virgin olive oil

2 tablespoons rinsed and chopped fresh parsley

1 tablespoon lemon zest

1 anchovy, mashed (optional)

Salt

Parmesan cheese, grated

1. Bring a large pot of water to boil. Add pasta and cook until al dente, approximately 5 minutes. Drain pasta in a colander and return to pot.

2. Drizzle with olive oil until lightly coated. Add parsley, lemon zest, and anchovy (if desired). Stir until combined. Season with salt to taste. Spoon into a bowl, sprinkle with Parmesan cheese, and serve.

Cooked pasta is best reheated in a microwave oven, which will not toughen it. Microwave the pasta covered at full power for 1 minute. Check the temperature, and then continue to reheat at 30-second intervals.

Penne with Broccoli Florets and Chickpeas

There are many kinds of frozen vegetables available in supermarkets that can be quickly microwaved. Broccoli is a popular one, but spinach works well, too. Chickpeas or cannellini beans taste best with pasta.

Makes 4 to 6 servings.

1 lb penne (regular or whole grain)

Extra virgin olive oil

1 12-oz bag broccoli florets, cooked to tender

1 10-oz can garbanzo beans (chickpeas), drained and rinsed

1 tablespoon lemon zest

Salt to taste

Parmesan cheese, grated

1. Bring a large pot of water to boil. Add pasta and cook until al dente, approximately 5 minutes. Drain pasta in a colander and return to pot.

2. Drizzle with olive oil until lightly coated. Add broccoli, beans, and lemon zest. Stir until combined with heat on Low until warmed through. Season with salt to taste. Sprinkle with Parmesan cheese, and serve.

When we think about vitamin C, citrus fruits usually come to mind. But a serving of broccoli contains more than 200 percent of the recommended daily allowance for vitamin C. No wonder it's considered a "wonder" food!

Italian Mushrooms with Meat Sauce

The Portobello mushrooms in this dish make it taste deceptively rich.

Makes 6 servings.

2 tablespoon olive oil, divided

1 lb ground turkey

2 tablespoons butter

2 cloves garlic, minced

¾ lb Portobello mushrooms, stemmed and sliced

½ lb domestic mushrooms, stemmed and sliced

½ teaspoon dried thyme

2½ cups low-fat chicken broth

2 teaspoons arrowroot

¼ cup low-fat half-and-half

Salt

Fresh parsley for garnish

1. Heat 1 tablespoon olive oil in a large skillet over medium-high heat. Add ground turkey and, using a fork to break it up, cook until browned throughout. Using a slotted spoon, transfer the meat to the slow cooker.

2. Wipe the residual oil off the skillet. Add the remaining tablespoon and the butter to the skillet. Over medium-high heat, add the garlic, mushrooms, and thyme. Cook until mushrooms are soft, about 10 minutes.

3. Add mushroom mix to the slow cooker with the broth. Cover and cook on Low for 6 to 8 hours or on High for 3 to 4 hours, until combination is tender. In a small bowl, stir the arrowroot into the half-and-half, and pour over mushrooms and meat.

4. Cover and cook an additional 15 to 20 minutes on high. The sauce should be bubbling and slightly thickened when ready to serve. Season with salt to taste. Serve over the pasta of your choice, and garnish with fresh parsley.

Portobello mushrooms originated in Portobello, Italy. The Portobello mushroom is essentially a larger, earthier variation on the basic domestic mushroom, which is why it's acceptable on a low-acid diet.

Ginger Chicken and Broccoli

This is an Asian-inspired sauce that is delicious on orzo, or can be served over brown rice or quinoa. Thigh meat is nice for sauces, as it yields more juice in the slow cooker.

6 boneless skinless chicken thighs, sliced into thick strips

2 tablespoons grated gingerroot

2 carrots, peeled and sliced into thin rounds

1 medium white onion, cut into thin wedges

1 red bell pepper, cored and seeded, sliced into thin strips

1 bag (1 lb) frozen sliced peaches, thawed

½ cup low-sodium soy sauce

¼ cup water

1 22-oz bag of frozen broccoli florets, thawed (approximately 5 cups)

1 small can of Chinese miniature corns, drained and rinsed (optional)

¼ cup water

2 tablespoons rice flour or arrowroot for use as a thickener

Non-stick cooking spray

1. Spray slow cooker with cooking spray. Place chicken in cooker; top with gingerroot, carrots, onion, peppers, and thawed peaches. In a small bowl, mix soy sauce and water. Pour over the chicken mixture. Cover and cook on Low for 6 to 7 hours or on High for 3 to 4 hours.

2. Remove lid and stir in thawed broccoli and miniature corns. In small bowl, combine the remaining ¼ cup water and the rice flour or arrowroot. Mix thoroughly, then stir into the chicken mixture. Replace the cover and put the heat on high. Cook an additional 15 to 20 minutes or until the sauce is bubbly and thickened. Serve over pasta, rice, or another grain.

The miniature corn sold in the international section of the grocery store is, in fact, real miniature corn. It has not been modified in any way, just picked when the cobs are still small. The cans in the store are imported from Asia, but more farmers are harvesting "baby" corn themselves, so keep an eye out for it at your farmer's market.

Confetti Chicken

This hearty yet low-fat combo will melt in your mouth.

Makes 6 servings.

6 boneless skinless chicken thighs, sliced into thick strips

1 tablespoon butter

1 medium white onion, chopped

½ lb domestic mushrooms, stemmed and sliced

½ red bell pepper, cored and seeded, sliced into strips

1 teaspoon fresh thyme

1½ cups low-fat chicken broth

1 15-oz can baby peas, drained

½ can (8 oz) low-sodium corn, drained

Salt to taste

Non-stick cooking spray

1. Spray slow cooker with cooking spray. Place chicken strips in cooker.

2. In skillet over medium-high heat, cook onion, mushrooms, and red pepper in butter until mushrooms are softened, about 10 minutes. Put mushroom/pepper mixture over chicken in slow cooker. Sprinkle fresh thyme over everything, then add the chicken broth.

3. Cover and cook on Low for 6 to 7 hours or on High for 3 to 4 hours. Uncover and add peas and corn, stirring to combine. Cover and cook on High an additional 10 to 15 minutes. Season with salt to taste. Serve over pasta or another grain.

If you're in a real rush, you can substitute a bag of mixed vegetables for the mélange of peppers, mushrooms, peas, and corn in this recipe. To do so, cook the onion, then add the bag of vegetables. Stir to coat them with the onion mixture, and proceed as directed.

Hearty Turkey and Veggie Sauce

While carrots, mushrooms, and red peppers shine in this thick sauce, the turkey adds texture and additional protein.

Makes 6 servings.

3 tablespoons olive oil

1 lb lean ground turkey

1 lb carrots, peeled and cut into small rounds

½ teaspoon dry thyme

1 teaspoon dried leaf basil

1 bay leaf

½ teaspoon oregano

1 teaspoon salt, or to taste

½ cup chopped white onion

1 clove garlic, crushed

1 red bell pepper, seeded and chopped

4 oz domestic mushrooms, sliced

¼ cup water

Parmesan cheese (optional)

1. In a skillet over medium-high heat, cook turkey in the olive oil. Saute until the turkey is browned through. While turkey is cooking, put carrots, thyme, basil, bay leaf, and oregano in slow cooker. Stir well, sprinkle with salt, and begin cooking on Low heat.

2. When turkey is browned, transfer to slow cooker with slotted spoon.

3. In pan drippings, sauté onion, garlic, pepper, and mushrooms until softened. Add this mixture to the slow cooker, and add ¼ cup of water. Cover and cook on Low 4 to 6 hours, or on High for 3 hours. Serve over the pasta of your choice, and sprinkle with Parmesan cheese if desired.

> **Feel free to substitute ground chicken for this recipe. Chicken and turkey are both excellent sources of low-fat protein.**

Eggplant, Squash, and Peppers

The addition of chicken to the eggplant-based sauce gives this tomato-less ratatouille some additional chewiness—and lots of flavor. The fresh basil added at the finish puts it over the top!

Makes 4 servings.

1½ cups cubed eggplant

½ cup coarsely chopped yellow summer squash or zucchini

½ cup coarsely chopped red pepper

¼ cup finely chopped white onion

2 tablespoons olive oil

¼ teaspoon salt

1 clove garlic, minced

2 chicken thighs, bone in, cooked separately

1 tablespoon fresh basil, coarsely chopped

Parmesan cheese

1. Combine eggplant, squash, pepper, onion, olive oil, salt, and garlic, and put in the slow cooker. Cover and cook on Low heat for 4 to 5 hours, or on High for 2 to 3 hours.

2. When ready to serve, break up chicken thighs and remove bones, stirring meat into the sauce. Add the chopped basil.

3. Serve over your favorite pasta, and sprinkle with Parmesan cheese.

A more traditional recipe for ratatouille contains green peppers. Because these have a higher pH than red peppers, they are not recommended for a low-acid diet. It's fortunate that the colorful and tasty red pepper has a lower pH and, therefore, is an acceptable low-acid diet food.

Squash "Stew" with Ground Meat

Makes 6 servings.

3 tablespoons extra-virgin olive oil

1 medium white onion, thinly sliced

1 clove garlic, sliced

1 lb ground chicken or turkey

1½ cups dried chickpeas, rinsed

1 medium-sized butternut squash, peeled and cut into large pieces

1 bunch Swiss chard, stems separated from the leaves, and both coarsely chopped

2 medium zucchini, cut into rounds

7 cups water

Parmesan cheese (optional)

1. Heat the olive oil in a large skillet over medium-high heat, and cook the onion and garlic until translucent, about 5 minutes. Add the ground meat and continue cooking until meat is browned.

2. In the slow cooker, place the chickpeas, squash, chard stems (not the leaves), zucchini, and salt. Add the sautéed meat mixture with the pan drippings, and top with 7 cups water . Stir, cover, and cook on Low for 7 to 8 hours.

3. Just before serving, lift the lid and stir in the chard leaves; cover and continue cooking 10 more minutes. Season with salt, and sprinkle with Parmesan cheese if desired.

Using dried chickpeas in this recipe ensures they don't get overly mushy with the extended cooking time. If you don't have dried chickpeas on hand, you can substitute a 16-ounce can. Add it toward the end of the cooking time.

Asian-Inspired Salmon

Try this warming and wonderful sauce on whole grain shells to get a real seaside feeling.

Makes 4 servings.

1 bag (1 lb) frozen sliced peaches, thawed

1 22-oz bag of frozen broccoli florets, thawed (approximately 5 cups)

2 tablespoons grated ginger

1 medium white onion, cut into thin slices

½ cup low-sodium soy sauce

½ cup water

4 salmon steaks, bones removed but skin on

1. Spray the slow cooker with cooking spray. Put in thawed peaches, thawed broccoli, ginger, and onion slices.

2. In a small bowl, mix soy sauce and water, and pour over the peach/broccoli mixture. Cover and cook on Low for 3 to 4 hours or on High for 2 to 3 hours.

3. Remove lid and place salmon pieces on top. Replace the lid and continue cooking for about an hour, until salmon is cooked through. Put on High and cook an additional 15 to 20 minutes or until the sauce is bubbly.

4. Serve over hot, cooked shells.

Many a cook has suffered a scraped knuckle while grating fresh ginger. If the ginger knob is large, peel only the amount you think you'll need and hold on to the remainder. If you're down to a small part, impale it on a fork and use that as your grating handle.

Asparagus with Shrimp and Toasted Sesame Seeds

This dish is great over angel hair pasta. It is fresh and flavorful, with a nice toasty crunch from the sesame seeds.

Makes 6 servings.

1 lb fresh asparagus, with tough bottoms removed, tips cut off and set aside, and stalks cut into ½-inch pieces

8 oz clam juice

8 oz low-fat chicken broth

1 lb (about 20) medium-sized raw shrimp, deveined and tails removed

2 teaspoons sesame seeds, toasted

2 tablespoons fresh herbs such as parsley, tarragon, dill and/or basil

1 tablespoons lemon zest

1. Into slow cooker, put asparagus, clam juice, and chicken broth. Cover and cook on Low for 3 to 4 hours or on High for 1 to 2 hours. Uncover and place shrimp on top of asparagus. Recover and continue to cook 30 minutes on Low or 15 minutes on high, until shrimp are pink and cooked through.

2. Preheat oven to 400F. Put sesame seeds on a baking sheet, and put in the oven. Toast for 5 to 10 minutes or until seeds are lightly browned. Remove pan from oven and let seeds cool.

3. Stir in fresh herbs and lemon zest. Serve, sprinkling with toasted sesame seeds.

Devein means to remove the black vein, actually the intestinal tract, from the shrimp. Do this with the tip of a sharp paring knife or with a specialized tool called a *deveiner*.

Monkfish with Capers, Eggplant, and Peppers

A firm white fish like monkfish is a great addition to the eggplant and pepper "stew." The capers add a peppery taste. If you don't like them, leave them out.

Makes 4 servings.

1 tablespoons butter

1 lb fresh monkfish, cut into cubes

1½ cups cubed eggplant

½ cup coarsely chopped red pepper

¼ cup finely chopped white onion

2 tablespoons olive oil

¼ teaspoon salt

1 clove garlic, minced

1 teaspoon lemon zest

1 tablespoon capers (optional)

Parmesan cheese (optional)

1. In a skillet, melt butter and add monkfish, and sauté just until it starts to turn white, about 3 minutes.

2. In a slow cooker, combine eggplant, pepper, onion, olive oil, salt, and garlic. Cover and cook on Low for 3 to 4 hours or on High for about 2 hours.

3. Uncover the cooker and add the monkfish and lemon zest. Replace the lid and continue to cook another hour on Low or about 30 minutes on High, until the fish is cooked through and white. When ready to serve, add the capers and stir until mixed through. Sprinkle with Parmesan cheese, if desired.

Seeing the beautiful white filets of the monkfish, you'd never suspect that they came from one of the ugliest fish in the sea! Monkfish have huge mouths and heads to help them bottom-feed. They were once called the poor man's lobster, then became overfished in the late 1990s and had to have their populations rebuilt. With careful management, the monkfish's population levels are now above normal.

Rib-Sticking Potato 'n Cabbage Sauce

If you're in the mood for something comforting and filling, look no further than this hearty combination of potatoes and cabbage, flavored with fresh sage.

Makes 4 servings.

⅓ cup olive oil

⅓ cup white onion, finely chopped

1 clove garlic, minced

1 medium-sized Yukon Gold potato, peeled and cut into strips

1 carrot, peeled and cut into matchstick strips

1 cup Savoy cabbage, shredded

6 fresh sage leaves, or 1 teaspoon dried sage

½ cup water

Parmesan cheese (optional)

1. Heat olive oil in a skillet on medium-high heat. Add onions and garlic and cook until translucent, about 5 minutes.

2. Put the potatoes and carrots in the slow cooker, and cover with the onion mixture. Next, add the cabbage and sage. Top with the water.

3. Cover the cooker and cook on Low for 4 to 5 hours or on High for 2 to 3 hours until the veggies are soft.

4. Serve over your favorite pasta, and sprinkle with Parmesan cheese if desired.

Choose a pasta that allows for plenty of surface area for the sauce created by this recipe. These include farfalle (bow ties), gemelli (twists), rotelle (wagon wheels), and orchiette (small shells).

Mushroom, Spinach, and Squash Medley

The mushrooms are the real stars of this dish, supported by the greens and squash. You can substitute summer squashes for the butternut squash for a winning summertime meal.

Makes 6 servings.

⅓ cup olive oil

1 clove garlic, minced

¼ lb domestic mushrooms, stems removed, thinly sliced

¼ lb Portobello mushrooms, stems removed, thinly sliced

Salt to taste

2 cups butternut squash, peeled, seeds removed, and cut into cubes

¼ cup water

3 cups packed fresh baby spinach leaves, chopped

Parmesan cheese (optional)

1. Heat olive oil in a skillet on medium-high heat. Add garlic and cook until it sizzles, 2 to 3 minutes. Add the mushrooms and sauté until just soft, about 5 minutes. Season with salt.

2. Put the mushroom mixture in the slow cooker, then add the butternut squash. Top with the water.

3. Cover the cooker and cook on Low for 5 to 6 hours or on High for 3 to 4 hours until the squash is soft and mushrooms are fragrant. Add the baby spinach, stir thoroughly, and put the cover back on. Turn the heat to Low and cook for another 10 to 15 minutes.

4. Serve over your favorite pasta, and sprinkle with Parmesan cheese if desired.

This is another recipe where the addition of some crisp-cooked prosciutto can enhance all the flavors. If you agree, take three or four slices of thinly sliced prosciutto, remove all fat, dice the meat, and sauté on medium-high heat for several minutes to get it crispy and cook off any remaining fat. Add as a topping to the dish.

Moroccan-Inspired Eggplant

Makes 4 servings.

⅓ cup olive oil

2 cloves garlic, minced

1 large eggplant, cubed

1 small cauliflower, coarse stems removed and cut into florets

1 tablespoons cumin

1 teaspoon turmeric

Salt to taste

¼ cup water

2 cups kale or Swiss chard, chopped (optional)

Parmesan cheese (optional)

1. Heat olive oil in a large skillet on medium-high heat. Add garlic and cook until it sizzles, 2 to 3 minutes. Add the eggplant and cauliflower and stir to coat with the hot oil and garlic. Add the cumin and turmeric, season with salt to taste, and sauté another 2 minutes.

2. Put the vegetable mixture in the slow cooker. Top with the water.

3. Cover the cooker and cook on Low for 5 to 6 hours or on High for 3 to 4 hours until the vegetables are soft. Add the kale or chard, stir thoroughly, and put the cover back on. Turn the heat to Low and cook for another 10 to 15 minutes.

4. Serve over your favorite pasta, and sprinkle with Parmesan cheese if desired.

The gold-colored spice turmeric, from the Indian plant *Curcuma longa*, contains a substance called *curcumin* that gives the spice its intense color. It turns out that it is also the element that makes turmeric one of the spices on the top of the health charts. Curcumin has been shown to have these properties: antioxidant, anti-inflammatory, antiviral, antibacterial, antifungal, and anticancer. It can also protect against diabetes, allergies, arthritis, Alzheimer's disease, and other chronic illnesses.

Zucchini Corn "Chowder" Sauce

An easy-to-make, fragrant summer "chowder" that is especially good with quinoa or couscous and a great accompaniment to grilled (skinless) chicken.

Makes 4 servings.

4 carrots, peeled and cut into 2-inch pieces

2 Yukon Gold potatoes, peeled and cut into cubes

1 red pepper, seeded and cut into cubes

1 white onion, finely chopped

2 cloves garlic, minced

1 cup vegetable broth

1 teaspoon kosher salt

1 medium zucchini, washed and sliced

1 16-oz can low-sodium sweet corn kernels, drained

Non-stick cooking spray

1. Spray the slow cooker liberally with non-stick cooking spray.

2. Combine the carrots, potatoes, red pepper, onion, garlic, broth, and salt in the slow cooker.

3. Cover and cook on Low for 5 to 6 hours or on High for 3 to 4 hours. Uncover, add the zucchini and corn, replace the cover, and cook on Low for another hour or so.

4. Serve over a hearty grain like brown rice or quinoa or over a delicate pasta like couscous.

This is a summer veggie delight. Make it in August, and you can use super-fresh zucchini and peppers and substitute fresh corn for canned corn.

Cannellini with Broccoli Rabe

Broccoli rabe served over orchietta pasta is a classic Italian dish. Adding white beans to this recipe enhances the nutritional value, texture, and taste.

Makes 4 servings.

2 tablespoons olive oil

4 cloves garlic, minced

1 large bunch broccoli rabe, rinsed, with coarsest parts of stems removed, and coarsely chopped (or 1 large head broccoli prepared similarly)

¼ teaspoon salt

1½ cups vegetable broth or reduced-sodium chicken broth

1 tablespoons flour

1 19-oz can cannellini beans, drained and rinsed

Parmesan cheese (optional)

1. Heat olive oil in a large skillet on medium-high heat. Add garlic and cook until it sizzles, 2 to 3 minutes. Add the broccoli rabe or broccoli florets and stir to coat with the hot oil and garlic. Season with salt.

2. Put the vegetable mixture in the slow cooker. Top with the broth.

3. Cover the cooker and cook on Low for 5 to 6 hours or on High for 3 to 4 hours until the vegetables are soft. Add the cannellini beans, stir thoroughly, and put the cover back on. Turn the heat to Low and cook for another 30 minutes until the beans are heated through.

4. Serve over your favorite pasta, and sprinkle with Parmesan cheese if desired.

When it comes to certain foods, what's in a name? Turns out *broccoli rabe* is no relation to broccoli. Rather, it's a descendant of a wild herb and a relative of the turnip. It's grown and used around the world, and is called many things, including raab, rapa, rapini, turnip broccoli, Italian or Chinese broccoli, Italian turnip, and broccoli de rabe.

Asian-Inspired Escarole

Another hearty green-based sauce that is especially good with a grain such as brown rice, quinoa, or bulgur.

Makes 4 servings.

¼ cup extra-virgin olive oil

4 cloves garlic (crushed or finely chopped)

2 bunches escarole, washed and coarsely chopped

2 teaspoons low-sodium soy sauce

2 teaspoons lemon zest

¼ teaspoon grated nutmeg, or slightly more if using a jarred spice

¼ cup vegetable broth

2 egg yolks

1 cup grated Parmesan cheese

1. Heat olive oil in a skillet on medium-high heat. Add garlic and cook until it sizzles, 2 to 3 minutes. Add the escarole and sauté until just coated with the oil and garlic, about 2 minutes. Season with salt.

2. Put the greens in the slow cooker, then add the soy sauce, lemon zest, and nutmeg. Top with the broth. Cover the cooker and cook on Low for 3 to 4 hours or on High for 1 to 2 hours until the greens are cooked through but not too mushy.

3. In a small bowl, beat the egg yolks until pale, and slowly pour over the hot escarole mixture, stirring continuously. Put the cover back on, turn the heat to Low and cook for another 10 minutes.

4. Serve over a hearty grain, and sprinkle with Parmesan cheese, if desired.

The combination of soy sauce, nutmeg, and lemon zest give this simple dish a real complexity. That's why it's particularly tasty served over a more neutral grain like quinoa or couscous.

Chapter 5

Poultry Is Your Low-Acid Friend

*C*hicken and turkey are protein sources that can be readily eaten by sufferers of reflux. They can be served baked, sautéed, or boiled—but never fried—and should have the skins removed before preparation. You can find skinless cuts of chicken in most grocery stores, which can save you time. Because chicken and turkey are such staples of a low-acid diet, though, you want to take some care to buy meat that is as high-quality as possible. Look for farm-raised chicken from a reputable source, such as a farmer at a local farmer's market, or select the least-processed meat from the supermarket.

Chicken with Mixed Vegetables

This is a great meal to throw together the night before when you have an especially busy day ahead. Prepare everything for the next day's extended time in the slow cooker tonight following these instructions and, instead of placing ingredients directly into the slow cooker, put them in a baking pan, where they can stay overnight in the refrigerator. In the morning, prep the slow cooker, transfer all the ingredients from the baking pan to the cooker, secure the top, set the heat, and let it cook. If you are making the dish for eating later the same day, just put the ingredients in the slow cooker as you prep them.

Makes 6 servings.

1 whole chicken cut into pieces, skin removed (or 6 chicken pieces of your choice)

1 tablespoons olive oil

1 small white onion, minced

1 clove garlic, minced

2 10-oz packages frozen mixed vegetables (almost any combination so long as the vegetables are not in a sauce)

3 tablespoons fresh parsley, chopped

1 tablespoon fresh rosemary, chopped

1 bay leaf

2 cups low-sodium chicken broth

Salt to taste

1. Preheat the oven broiler, and line a pan with heavy-duty aluminum foil. Rinse chicken and pat dry with paper towels. Broil chicken pieces for 3 minutes a side, until browned. Transfer chicken pieces to the slow cooker.

2. Heat oil in a skillet over medium-high heat, and add onions and garlic, cooking until onions are translucent, about 3 minutes. Scrape mixture over chicken.

3. Add frozen vegetables, parsley, rosemary, bay leaf, and chicken broth, and stir everything together.

4. When the ingredients are in the slow cooker, cover and set to Low. Cook for 7 to 8 hours. Chicken and vegetables will be cooked through. Remove bay leaf, season with salt, and serve.

Vary and intensify this recipe with a couple of last-minute additions. When ready to serve, stir in a teaspoon of cumin. In a glass measuring cup, combine 1 tablespoon water with 1 tablespoon arrowroot or cornstarch, and mix together to form a paste. Add about a half cup of the hot juices from this dish and stir briskly to combine. Add another half cup or so of hot juices, mix, then return the mixture to the slow cooker. Cover and cook another 10 minutes or so to thicken.

Ginger-Soy Chicken

An Asian-inspired, delightfully easy dish to make—and you may even pretend you're eating General Tso's Chicken at a Chinese restaurant!

Makes 4 servings.

⅓ cup lite soy sauce

2 tablespoons dark-brown sugar

3 garlic cloves, thinly sliced

⅔ cup fresh cilantro, chopped, plus sprigs for garnish

1 piece fresh ginger (about 2 inches long), peeled and cut into thin strips

1 teaspoon balsamic vinegar

1 teaspoon ground coriander

2½ lb chicken pieces, bone in, skin removed

2 medium carrots, peeled and thinly sliced crosswise

1 10-oz bag frozen broccoli florets

1 tablespoon rice flour or arrowroot (to use as a thickener)

Rice (as bedding)

Cilantro (as garnish)

1. In the slow cooker, stir together the soy sauce, sugar, garlic, cilantro, ginger, vinegar, and coriander. Add chicken, carrots, and broccoli; toss to coat. Cover and cook on Low for 5 to 7 hours or on High for 3 to 4 hours, until chicken is cooked through and tender.

2. Using a large spoon, skim off and discard any fat from surface of cooking liquid.

3. In a 2-cup glass measuring cup, whisk rice flour or arrowroot with 1 tablespoon water. Add 1 cup of the liquid from the cooked chicken, and whisk to combine. Pour into a small saucepan, and bring to a boil. Stirring often, cook the mixture until thickened, about 1 minute. Turn off the slow cooker and stir in the cornstarch mixture.

4. Serve over rice (brown rice is best), and garnish with the cilantro.

> If you're a fan of dark meat chicken, choose a package that's all thighs. Remember to remove the skin, though.

Turkey Tonnato

This is a favorite summer dish, as cooking the turkey in the slow cooker means the kitchen doesn't get hot. The chilled turkey in the tuna sauce is a delicious combination.

Makes 4 servings.

2 lb boneless, skinless turkey breast

2 cloves garlic, cut into thick slices

1½ cups low-sodium chicken broth

Small white onion, sliced

½ cup water

Carrot, peeled and sliced

4 sprigs fresh parsley

2 sprigs fresh thyme

Bay leaf

Salt to taste

2 5-oz cans Albacore tuna in water

2 tablespoons anchovy paste

¼ cup lite mayonnaise

2 tablespoons capers, drained and rinsed

1. Place turkey breasts between two sheets of plastic wrap. Pound with the flat side of a meat mallet or the bottom of a small saucepan until the meat is a uniform thickness and looks like a large, thick pancake. Roll the meat into a shape that will fit into the slow cooker, and tie with kitchen string. Make about 10 slits in the meat and insert a garlic sliver into each one.

2. Place turkey breast in the slow cooker; add broth, onion, water, carrot, parsley, thyme, and bay leaf; and sprinkle lightly with salt. Cover and cook on Low for 6 to 8 hours or on High for 3 to 4 hours. The turkey should be cooked through, with the juices running clear. Remove the turkey from the cooker, allow to cool slightly, then refrigerate to chill.

3. Make the sauce by combining tuna and anchovy paste in a food processor or blender until smooth. Scrape into a bowl and add the mayonnaise and capers, stirring to combine.

4. To serve, remove and discard the kitchen string. Thinly slice the turkey, and spoon some sauce over it. Pass additional sauce separately.

> Although there is no use for the braising liquid in this recipe, it's a richly flavored stock and it's a shame to throw it away. Freeze it and use it in place of chicken stock when cooking another recipe.

Chicken with Cauliflower, Lentils, and Chickpeas

A mouth-watering combination of super-nutritious beans, with succulent vegetables.

Makes 6 servings.

3 tablespoons olive oil

3 cloves garlic, minced

2-inch piece fresh ginger, minced

3 cups low-sodium chicken broth

2 cups low-fat plain yogurt

6 chicken thighs, bone-in and skinless

Salt

1 lb bag brown lentils, picked over

1 head cauliflower, broken into large florets

2 16-oz cans chickpeas, drained and rinsed

Bunch fresh cilantro leaves, chopped

1. Heat oil in a large skillet over medium-high heat. Cook the garlic and ginger, stirring, until fragrant, about 2 minutes.

2. Put the chicken broth in the slow cooker and add the ginger/garlic mixture. Stir to combine well, and then add the yogurt, continuing to stir to combine.

3. Lightly season the chicken with some salt, and put in the slow cooker. Add the lentils. Cover and cook on Low for 7 to 10 hours or on High for 5 to 6 hours. Add the cauliflower and chickpeas about halfway through cooking, whether on High or Low.

4. Serve over bowls of warm rice, garnishing with cilantro.

Lentils are much more commonly used in the cuisines of Europe and the Middle East. They are part of the legume family, making them high in protein and fiber—a great substitute for meat. They are also loaded with folate, iron, phosphorous, potassium, and fiber. They provide a tasty, simple—and economical— alternative to meat.

Arroz con Pollo

Yes, you can have a Spanish-style chicken-and-rice dish without tomatoes, olives, and wine. Replacing hot spices with aromatic spices allows you to add flavor without triggering heartburn.

Makes 4 servings.

3 to 4 lbs of chicken pieces, preferably drumsticks and thighs, skin removed

4 tablespoons olive oil

1 large white onion, diced

2 cloves garlic, minced

1 red bell pepper, seeds and ribs removed, and diced

1 teaspoon paprika

1 teaspoon ground cumin

2 teaspoon dried oregano

2 cups low-fat chicken broth

1 bay leaf

1 cup uncooked converted long-grain rice

1 10-oz bag frozen peas

Salt to taste

1. Preheat the oven broiler. Line a broiler pan with heavy-duty aluminum foil. Broil the chicken pieces for about 3 minutes on each side, until browned.

2. Heat 2 tablespoons of the oil in a medium skillet over medium-high heat. Add onion, garlic, and red pepper, and cook, stirring, until onion is translucent, about 4 minutes. Reduce the heat to Low, add the paprika, cumin, and oregano, and cook for another minute or so, stirring constantly. Scrape mixture into the slow cooker.

3. Add chicken broth and bay leaf and stir well. Cover and cook on Low for 4 to 6 hours or on High for 2 to 3 hours, until chicken is nearly cooked through.

4. While chicken is cooking, add the remaining 2 tablespoons of oil to the skillet. Add the rice and, while stirring, cook for 3 to 4 minutes, until grains are opaque and lightly browned. Remove the pan from the heat and set aside.

5. If cooking on low, raise the heat to high. Add the rice to the slow cooker and cook another hour until the rice is almost tender and chicken is cooked through and tender. Add the peas and cook another 10 to 15 minutes.

6. Remove and discard bay leaf, season with salt, and serve.

It's important for the success of this dish and other dishes that include rice that you use long-grain converted rice. A shorter-grain rice will turn to mush. Converted white rice has undergone a steam-pressure process that makes the grains fluffier and helps keep them separated when cooked.

Chicken and Mushroom Stew

The combination of domestic and Portobello mushrooms, along with carrots and celery, make for an earthy, satisfying stew. Serve over rice, bulgur, or quinoa.

Makes 4 servings.

1½ lb chicken pieces, boneless and skinless
½ lb domestic mushrooms
½ lb Portobello mushrooms
2 tablespoons butter
1 small white onion, chopped
2 cloves garlic, minced
2 carrots, peeled and sliced thin
1 celery rib, sliced
1½ cups low-fat chicken broth
2 tablespoons fresh parsley, chopped
1 tablespoons fresh thyme, chopped
Salt to taste

1. Trim any fat from the chicken pieces and cut into 1-inch cubes. Rinse mushrooms lightly, discard stems, and cut the domestic mushrooms in half and the Portobello mushrooms into chunks.

2. Heat the butter in a medium skillet over medium-high heat. Add the onion and garlic and cook, stirring, until onion is translucent, about 3 minutes. Add the mushrooms and cook, stirring frequently, for another 3 or 4 minutes until mushrooms begin to soften. Scrape mixture into the slow cooker.

3. Add the chicken, carrots, celery, broth, parsley, and thyme. Stir to combine. Cover and cook on Low for 4 to 6 hours or on High for 2 to 3 hours until chicken is cooked through and vegetables are tender.

4. Season with salt and serve over rice.

> Heat and light are the two worst enemies of dried herbs and spices, so a pretty display rack over the stove is about the worst place to store them. Keep them in a cool, dark place to preserve their potency. Test for freshness with a quick sniff: If the aroma isn't strong, you need a new bottle.

Chicken and Clams

This surf-and-turf indulgence over linguini or thick spaghetti will have you coming back for more.

Makes 4 to 6 servings.

2 tablespoons olive oil

About 1 cup of all-purpose flour, for dredging

6 pieces of chicken, bone in and skinless

1 medium carrot, peeled and sliced

1 medium white onion, diced

1 tablespoon fresh ginger, peeled and minced

½ cup water

2 dozen littleneck clams, rinsed in several changes of water until water runs clear, and drained

Linguini or thick spaghetti

1. Heat the oil over medium-high heat in a large skillet. Put the flour in a pie plate or shallow bowl and season it with salt. Coat the chicken pieces with the flour, shaking off any excess, and put on a plate. When the oil is hot, put the chicken pieces in it. Cook the chicken, turning every so often, until the chicken is browned on all sides.

2. Put the chicken pieces in the slow cooker. Add the carrot, onion, ginger, and water. Cover and cook on Low for 4 to 5 hours.

3. Turn the heat to high so that the liquid is bubbling. Add the clams, replace the cover, and cook an additional 30 to 40 minutes, or until the clams are opened.

4. Serve over linguine or thick spaghetti.

> There are several varieties of clams on the market, and it can be confusing if you don't know much about them. Here's a lesson in simplicity: These three clams are the same, they just vary in size. The littleneck clam is the smallest, cooks the fastest, and is most tender. The cherry stone clam is the next size up. The quahog clam is the largest. These tougher, longer-cooking clams are typically used in chowders.

Chicken and Fennel

Using dark-meat chicken pieces (thighs) in this recipe better complements the light, licorice flavor of the fennel. Couscous is a wonderful accompaniment.

Makes 4 to 6 servings.

6 chicken thighs, bone in and skinless

1 tablespoon fennel seeds, crushed

1 teaspoon orange zest

Salt to taste

1 tablespoon olive oil

1 small white onion, cut into 8 wedges

1 large fennel bulb, trimmed and cut into 8 wedges

1½ lbs Yukon Gold potatoes, peeled and cut into 1-inch cubes

1. Place chicken pieces in the slow cooker, and sprinkle fennel seeds, orange zest, and salt to taste.

2. Add oil to a skillet and heat over medium-high heat. Add onion and cook until translucent, about 3 minutes, then add onion to the slow cooker.

3. Add fennel and potatoes to the slow cooker. Add water and stir to combine.

4. Cover and cook on Low for 6 to7 hours or on High for 3 to 4 hours until chicken is cooked through and vegetables are tender.

5. Serve with couscous.

Fennel is another delicious vegetable that you will want to have on hand for everything from improving the taste and texture of soups and stews to adding to salads and snacking on as you would a carrot. Its mellow licorice flavor is refreshing and clean. Fennel is a great source of fiber, vitamin C, folate, potassium, and manganese.

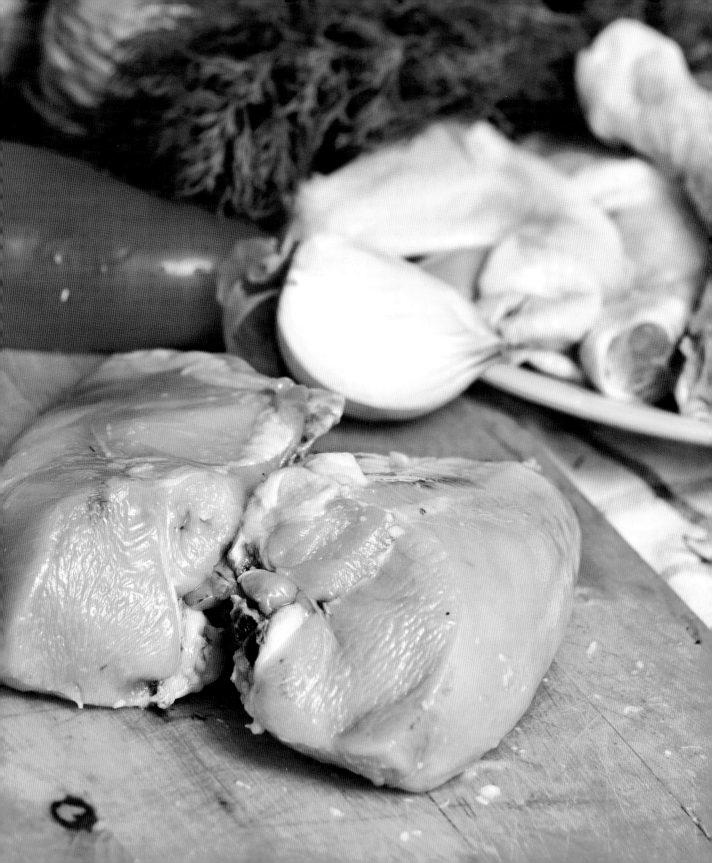

Chicken Thighs *a la Provence*

Travel to the south of France with this dish, which slow-cooks the chicken with basil, thyme, fennel, and a hint of orange.

Makes 6 servings.

3 teaspoons olive oil

1 large white onion, thinly sliced

2 cloves garlic, crushed with garlic press

2 red peppers, ribs and seeds removed, cut into strips

1 yellow pepper, ribs and seeds removed, cut into strips

2 lbs boneless chicken thighs, skin removed

¼ teaspoon dried thyme

¼ teaspoon fennel seeds, crushed

1 teaspoon orange zest

½ cup loosely packed basil leaves, chopped

½ cup water

1. In a large skillet, heat the olive oil and add the onion, garlic, and peppers. Cook, stirring, for 3 to 5 minutes until onion is translucent and peppers are soft.

2. Put chicken pieces into the slow cooker, and put the onions and peppers on top. Add the herbs, orange zest, and water, and stir to combine.

3. Cover and cook on Low for 6 to 7 hours or on High for 4 to 5 hours, or until chicken is tender and cooked through.

4. Serve with brown rice or whole wheat pasta.

Provence, in southern France, captures people's imaginations for the good life: sunshine; small, quaint villages; artists; and, of course, food. The colors and flavors are sun-drenched and pronounced. If you can't get there, find some images of the area that you particularly like, make this dish, and bask in the feeling.

Cornish Hens with Fresh Greens

Cornish hens are as easy to make as dishes with chicken pieces, but there's something about them that makes the meal seem extra-special. Served with quinoa, this dish makes a restaurant-caliber presentation.

Makes 4 servings.

2 tablespoons olive oil

1 small white onion, minced

1 garlic clove, minced

2 small Cornish game hens, split in two, skin removed

1 head Swiss chard, washed, coarse stems removed, and leaves chopped in large pieces

1 head Escarole, washed, trimmed, and chopped in large pieces

1 small package frozen spinach

½ cup low-sodium chicken broth

1. Heat oil in a small skillet over medium-high heat, and cook onions and garlic about 3 minutes, or until onion is translucent. Scrape mixture into slow cooker.

2. Place Cornish hens on top of onion mixture, and top with greens and broth.

3. Cover the slow cooker and cook on Low for 6 to 7 hours or on High for 4 to 5 hours, or until chicken is tender and cooked through and greens are soft and fragrant.

My mother used to make Cornish hens regularly. When you had a half of one of these on your plate, you felt like you were getting a lot of food—and they are fun to eat as you navigate the small sizes and bones.

Thai Chicken

Coconut milk, basil, and fish sauce combine to make a most fragrant and flavorful dish. A bowl of steaming rice noodles is the perfect accompaniment.

Makes 4 servings.

1 lb boneless, skinless chicken breast halves

3 tablespoons fish sauce

½ cup unsweetened coconut milk

1 tablespoon low-sodium soy sauce

1 tablespoon brown sugar

2 teaspoons canola oil

2 teaspoons fresh ginger, peeled and minced

1 clove garlic, crushed with a garlic press

1½ cups loosely packed fresh basil leaves, coarsely chopped

1. Using a sharp knife, cut the chicken breast halves into ¼-inch slices.

2. In a medium bowl, combine fish sauce, coconut milk, soy sauce, and brown sugar. Stir to combine thoroughly.

3. Put the chicken slices into the slow cooker, and top with the fish sauce mixture.

4. In a skillet over medium-high heat, add the oil and cook the ginger and garlic, stirring frequently, for about 2 minutes until fragrant. Add to the slow cooker.

5. Top with the basil leaves, and stir all ingredients. Cover and cook on Low 5 to 6 hours or on High 3 to 4 hours, until chicken is cooked through.

Frequently, coconut milk separates in the can with the liquid on the bottom and a thick layer of coconut on top. Whisk it briskly until the lumps are gone, because they will not break up well with the low heat in the slow cooker.

Turkey with Corn and Peppers

This is a colorful and energizing "goulash" that brings a bite of summer to whatever time of year you make it.

Makes 6 servings.

1 lb lean ground turkey

1 tablespoon olive oil

1 small white onion, diced

2 red peppers, ribs and seeds removed, diced

2 10-oz bags frozen corn kernels (with no sauces)

½ cup loosely packed basil leaves, coarsely chopped

½ cup low-sodium chicken broth

Non-stick cooking spray

1. Coat the inside of the slow cooker with non-stick cooking spray. Place the ground turkey on the bottom of the slow cooker.

2. In a skillet over medium-high heat, add the oil and cook the onion and red peppers, stirring frequently, for about 3 minutes until onion is translucent and peppers are just softening. Add this mixture to the slow cooker.

3. Pour the frozen corn kernels over everything, add the chopped basil, and top with the chicken broth.

4. Cover and cook on Low for 5 to 6 hours or on High for 3 to 4 hours or until meat is cooked through and vegetables are soft.

5. When cooked, break up meat at the bottom of the cooker with a large fork so it separates in chunks. Stir and serve.

Make lots of this in the late summer when these vegetables are fresh and plentiful, and freeze portions to heat up in the winter and late spring, when your body seems to ache for these amazing flavors.

Chickatouille

A twist on conventional ratatouille, this combines the fresh veggies the dish is known for with tasty chicken—oh, and without tomatoes! Serve over your favorite pasta.

Makes 4 to 6 servings.

6 chicken thighs, skin removed

1½ cups cubed eggplant

½ cup coarsely chopped yellow summer squash or zucchini

½ cup coarsely chopped red pepper

¼ cup finely chopped white onion

2 tablespoons olive oil

¼ teaspoon salt

1 clove garlic, minced

1 tablespoon fresh basil, coarsely chopped

Parmesan cheese

1. Put the chicken thighs in the bottom of the slow cooker. Combine the eggplant, squash, pepper, onion, olive oil, salt, and garlic and add to the chicken in the slow cooker. Cover and cook on Low for 4 to 5 hours or on High for 2 to 3 hours.

2. When ready to serve, break up chicken thighs and remove bones, stirring meat into the sauce.

3. Add the chopped basil.

4. Serve over your favorite pasta, and sprinkle with Parmesan cheese.

The basil in this recipe helps distinguish it as something with a Mediterranean twist. Basil's distinctive flavor is celebrated around the world. It is easy to grow, whether in a formal garden or a container garden. It is also a known digestive aid.

Stuffed Turkey Breast

This is a colorful dish, with a layer of bright green spinach and tasty prosciutto creating a spiral through the turkey.

Makes 6 servings.

1 2-lb boneless, skinless turkey breast half

1 10-oz package frozen chopped spinach, thawed

3 tablespoons low-fat milk

1 large egg

½ cup panko breadcrumbs

¼ lb prosciutto, with fat removed

2 cloves garlic, cut into 4 slivers each

2 cups low-sodium chicken broth

1 small white onion, sliced

1 carrot, peeled and sliced

4 sprigs fresh parsley

2 springs fresh thyme

1 bay leaf

1. Place turkey breast between two sheets of plastic wrap. Pound with the flat side of a meat mallet or the bottom of a small saucepan until it is a uniform thickness.

2. Place spinach in a colander and press with the back of a spoon to extract as much liquid as possible.

3. Combine milk, egg, and breadcrumbs in a mixing bowl, and whisk well. Stir in spinach.

4. Layer the prosciutto on top of the turkey breast, and spread spinach mixture on top. Roll turkey breast into a shape that will fit into your slow cooker, and tie with kitchen string. Make eight slits in the meat and insert slivers of garlic into them.

5. Place the turkey breast in the slow cooker, and add broth, onion, carrot, parsley, thyme, and bay leaf. Cover and cook on Low for 6 to 8 hours or on High for 3 to 4 hours, or until turkey is cooked through and juices run clear.

6. Remove turkey from the slow cooker and transfer to a platter. Cut and discard string. Remove and discard the bay leaf from the sauce. Thinly slice the turkey, and pour some sauce over the entire portion.

Pounding a piece of meat into a thinner and more uniform piece not only makes it convenient to stuff and roll, as is necessary in this recipe, but also tenderizes the meat. The pounding on the muscle fibers breaks them down. As long as your meat is carefully placed between sheets of strong plastic wrap that you won't break through by hitting on it too hard, it's also enjoyable to do.

Chicken-Stuffed Cabbage

These are cooked just long enough for the cabbage to get soft without getting too tender, which gives them great texture and taste. Serve with a piece of crusty French bread.

Makes 4 servings.

1 small head (about 1.5 lbs) green cabbage

1 lb ground chicken (or turkey)

1 cup cooked brown or white rice

1 small white onion, minced

½ teaspoon lemon zest

1 tablespoon fresh parsley, chopped fine

1 cup low-sodium chicken broth

Salt to taste

1. Bring a 4-quart saucepan of water to a boil. Remove core from cabbage by cutting around it with a sharp knife. Pull off 10 to 12 large leaves from the outside and set aside. Cut remaining cabbage in half, and cut off 2 cups of thin shreds. Blanch the large leaves and the shreds in the boiling water for 5 minutes, and then drain them.

2. Combine the ground chicken, cooked rice, onion, lemon zest, and parsley in a mixing bowl. Set aside.

3. Place half of the drained cabbage shreds into the bottom of the slow cooker. Make the stuffed cabbage leaves by placing ½ cup of the chicken mixture at the root end of a cabbage leaf then tucking in the sides and rolling the leaf up into a cylinder. Repeat until all leaves are filled.

4. Place the rolls seam side down in the slow cooker, layering gently if necessary. Add the chicken broth.

5. Cover and cook on Low for 8 to 10 hours or on High for 4 to 5 hours, until the sauce is bubbly and the chicken juices are running clear.

6. Serve with a piece of crusty French bread.

People have been eating cabbage for thousands of years. It grows well in cool climates, yields large harvests, and stays fresh through the winter, making it an excellent food source. It's a relative of broccoli, Brussels sprouts, cauliflower, and even kale and is loaded with fiber. The largest head of cabbage is credited to Englishman William Collingwood who, in 1865, produced one that weighed 123 pounds.

Chapter 6

Fish Dishes That Fulfill Wishes

*G*reat news: Fish is on the menu if you suffer from reflux! You can eat almost any fish, from flounder to salmon to tilapia to scallops—as well as shellfish such as clams, shrimp, and lobster. Always seek out the freshest fish possible, and choose wild fish over farm-raised fish. Just avoid frying.

If fish wasn't a big part of your diet before you started on a low-acid regime, you should challenge yourself to find recipes in this chapter that sound good to you and try to eat fish at least a couple of times a week. It may surprise you how much you actually like fish!

A Little Lemon, A Lot of Luvin'

Citrus fruits are at the top of the list of foods that those on low-acid diets should avoid. However, the zest from lemons and oranges can be added to recipes—in moderation—to add flavor, freshness, and vitamins.

Makes 4 servings.

1½ lbs fish filets (white fish like tilapia)

Salt to taste

1 medium white onion, chopped

5 tablespoons parsley, chopped

2 teaspoons lemon zest (finely grated rind)

2 teaspoons orange zest (finely grated rind)

4 teaspoons olive oil

Parsley (for garnish)

Non-stick cooking spray

1. Spray the inside of the slow cooker liberally with non-stick spray. Season the filets with salt, and place fish in the slow cooker.

2. Add the onion, parsley, lemon zest, orange zest, and oil. Cover and cook on Low for 1 to 2 hours.

3. Serve garnished with fresh parsley.

> How fortunate that a low-acid diet can be enhanced with the flavors of lemon and orange through the powerful oils in the zests of these fruits! Using the finest holes on a grater, and not going beyond the colorful peel, you can grate fresh zest to add to a number of recipes to add lots of flavor.

Fennel, Potato, and Mussel Melange

This dish is a hearty stew in which the mussels add their characteristic meaty succulence. With a salad of fresh greens on the side and some hearty sourdough bread, it makes a delightful meal.

Makes 4 servings.

4 cups low-sodium chicken broth

⅔ teaspoon saffron

¾ cup olive oil

1 medium white onion, chopped

1 garlic clove, minced

1 small fennel bulb, fronds removed, washed and cored, then chopped

3 Idaho potatoes, peeled and diced

3 lbs mussels, scrubbed and beards removed

1 tablespoon fresh parsley, chopped

1. Pour 1 cup of the broth into a small bowl (reserving 3 cups of broth) and add the saffron. Set aside.

2. Warm oil in a skillet over medium heat, and add onion and garlic. Cook, stirring, for about 3 minutes or until onions are translucent.

3. Put the onion mixture into the slow cooker, and add the fennel, potatoes, and the remaining 3 cups of chicken broth. Cover and cook on Low for 3 to 4 hours or on High for about 2 hours, or until vegetables are tender.

4. If cooking on Low, turn heat to High. Add saffron broth and mussels, cover, and cook an additional 30 to 50 minutes, until mussels are open.

5. Serve in bowls with pieces of hearty sourdough bread. Garnish liberally with parsley.

> Mussels are tender and delicious, and this recipe is full of flavor! Mussels should be fresh when you buy and eat them. Before purchasing, give a sniff. Mussels should smell like the ocean or a clean beach. If some are open, tap them with your finger. This triggers them to close. If they don't, they're not fresh. Mussels can be enjoyed year-round.

Bouillabaisse

This is an amazing one-pot meal of assorted fish and shellfish that's free of tomatoes but full of flavor. Serve with brown rice, saffron-infused Arborio rice (to make a paella of sorts), or with a hunk of fresh bread.

Makes 6 servings.

1 large white onion, chopped

3 cloves garlic, minced

2 large stalks celery, fronds removed, finely chopped

1 red pepper, seeded and chopped

8 oz clam juice

½ cup water

2 tablespoons extra virgin olive oil

1 tablespoon lemon zest

1 tablespoon fresh basil, chopped

1 tablespoon fresh parsley, chopped

½ teaspoon onion powder

1 teaspoon fresh oregano

1 teaspoon fresh thyme

1 bay leaf

¼ teaspoon sugar

1 lb. firm white fish, cut into 1-inch pieces

¾ lb shelled, cleaned shrimp, tails removed

½ lb squid, cleaned and sliced

6.5-oz can chopped clams and the juice

6-oz can crabmeat (or 8 oz cleaned, fresh crabmeat)

Salt to taste

¼ cup fresh parsley, chopped

Non-stick cooking spray

1. Spray the inside of the slow cooker with non-stick cooking spray. In a large bowl, combine onions, garlic, celery, red pepper, clam juice, water, olive oil, zest, spices, bay leaf, and sugar. Mix well. Put into slow cooker. Cover and cook on Low for 4 to 5 hours or on High for 2 to 3 hours until base is hot and flavors are combined.

2. If cooking on High, reduce heat to Low. Stir in fish, shrimp, squid, clams, and crab and cook for an additional 45 minutes to 1 hour or until fish is done. Remove bay leaf before serving. Stir in or garnish with parsley.

This classic French fish "boil" is said to have originated in the seaside town of Marseilles in the south of France. The word itself has a fanciful attribution—bouille-abbesse, or the abbess' boil—in reference to a particular Abbesse in a convent there; and the more practical bouillon abaissé, meaning, "to reduce by evaporation."

Zucchini-Ginger Fish

A simple dish, for sure, but you'll find the flavors meld beautifully. The fresh ginger is the key ingredient.

Makes 4 to 6 servings.

4 medium zucchini, sliced into
¼-inch rounds and then cut in
half to form half moons

1 tablespoons fresh ginger, grated

2 cloves garlic, minced

2 tablespoons water

3 lbs firm white fish, like mahimahi, cubed

Sprigs of fresh parsley

Non-stick cooking spray

1. Spray the inside of the slow cooker with non-stick cooking spray.

2. In a large bowl, combine zucchini, ginger, garlic, and water. Stir to combine and add to the slow cooker. Cook on Low for 3 to 4 hours or on High for about 2 hours.

3. Uncover; if you are cooking on High, reduce heat to Low; and add fish cubes. Cover again and cook an additional hour or longer, until fish is cooked through and tender. Garnish with the parsley.

Mahimahi are also called *Dolphinfish,* though they bear no relation to dolphins. They are considered one of the most beautiful fish in the sea, with brightly colored flanks. They can be found worldwide in tropical and subtropical waters. Mahimahi is prized for its sweet, mild flavor and large, tender flakes when cooked.

Catfish Gumbo

Like the recipe for seafood bouillabaisse, this one is a take on a traditional gumbo because it also doesn't feature tomatoes. Good tasting and good for you!

Makes 4 servings.

2 tablespoons olive oil

1 small white onion, chopped

1 clove garlic, minced

2 red bell peppers, seeded and cut into thin strips

1½ lbs okra, trimmed, and sliced into ½-inch rounds

1 teaspoon lemon zest

Salt

1 cup water

4 5-oz catfish filets

2 tablespoons fresh cilantro, chopped

Non-cooking spray

1. Spray the inside of the slow cooker with non-stick cooking spray. In a large skillet, heat the oil over medium-high heat, add the onion and garlic, and cook, stirring, for about 3 minutes or until onion is translucent. Add the red pepper strips and continue stirring for another minute.

2. Put mixture into slow cooker, add okra, zest, and salt to taste. Stir to combine, then top with water.

3. Cover and cook on Low for 5 to 6 hours or on High for 3 to 4 hours until vegetables are tender.

4. Reduce or keep heat to Low and add the fish filets. Cover and cook an additional 1 to 2 hours or until fish is cooked through and tender.

5. Serve sprinkled with fresh cilantro.

This south-of-the-border dish features the ingredient that's synonymous with gumbo: okra. It's a vegetable people tend to love or hate. It's the slimy consistency it can take on that tends to turn people off. To minimize that, bring the okra to room temperature an hour before you will cook with it. After cutting the vegetable into rounds, let it sit an additional 30 to 60 minutes to dry out some more.

Clam Sauce for Spaghetti

The recipe calls for canned clams, which are the heart of the sauce, but adding fresh clams or mussels will make it extra special and extra delicious. Serve over linguine or thick spaghetti.

Makes 4 servings.

2 4-oz cans clams

1 8-oz bottle clam juice

2 tablespoons olive oil

1 garlic clove, minced

1 teaspoon fresh ginger, grated

½ teaspoon lemon zest

Salt to taste

1 lb littleneck clams or mussels, if desired, scrubbed clean

2 tablespoons fresh parsley, chopped

1. In a large bowl, combine clams, clam juice, olive oil, garlic, ginger, and zest. Stir well. Add salt to taste.

2. Put mixture in slow cooker, cover, and cook on Low for 4 to 5 hours or on High for 3 to 4 hours.

3. If desired, add the clams or mussels, put heat on Low, cover, and cook an additional hour or so until shellfish opens.

4. Serve over bowls of thick spaghetti or linguine, and garnish with fresh parsley.

It's now possible to find fresh minced clams in just about every supermarket. If they're not in the refrigerated case, check the freezer. If you must resort to canned clams, use 3 (6.5-ounce) cans for each pint of fresh clams specified.

Trout with Mushrooms and Spinach

This tasty treat can be served warm over couscous, or chill it and place the filets over fresh greens, topping with some of the spinach/mushroom mixture for a lovely salad.

Makes 4 servings.

2 tablespoons olive oil

1 lb domestic mushrooms, rinsed, caps removed, and sliced

2 bags frozen spinach

Salt to taste

4 5-oz filets trout

Non-stick cooking spray

1. Spray the inside of the slow cooker with non-stick cooking spray.

2. In a medium skillet, heat the olive oil and add the mushrooms, cooking for about 2 minutes until coated and just turning.

3. Put frozen spinach in slow cooker. Add mushrooms and stir to combine. Season with salt.

4. Cover and cook on Low for 4 to 5 hours or on High for 2 to 3 hours, until mushrooms are tender.

5. Place trout filets over spinach, cover, and cook an additional hour on Low for 30 to 40 minutes on High until fish is cooked through and tender.

6. Serve over warm couscous—or chill and serve over salad greens.

> Trout is a freshwater fish that is closely related to salmon and char. It yields meaty filets that can be prepared in many styles. Be sure you buy the freshest trout possible. If there is an odor or sliminess, the fish is not fresh.

Calamari with Garbanzo Beans and Greens

The Swiss chard adds nice color to this Italian dish. Enjoy with a bowl of steaming brown rice.

Makes 4 to 6 servings.

1 large bunch Swiss chard, tough stems removed and chopped into 1-inch slices

1½ lbs squid, cleaned

¼ cup olive oil

1 medium white onion, diced

1 clove garlic, minced

1 carrot, peeled and chopped

1 cup seafood stock or low-sodium chicken broth

2 tablespoons fresh parsley, chopped

1 teaspoon dried oregano

1 15-oz can garbanzo beans, drained and rinsed

Salt to taste

1. Bring a large pot of water to boil, and have a bowl of ice water handy. Boil Swiss chard leaves for about 2 minutes, then drain and plunge into ice water to stop the cooking action. Drain again, and transfer Swiss chard to the slow cooker.

2. Rinse the squid inside and out. Cut bodies into ¾-inch rings, leaving tentacles whole. Set aside.

3. Heat oil in a medium skillet over medium-high heat. Add onion, garlic, and carrot, and cook, stirring frequently, for about 5 minutes or until onion softens. Add broth, parsley, and oregano. Bring to a boil over high heat. Pour mixture into slow cooker.

4. Add squid to the slow cooker, and stir well. Cook on Low for 2 to 4 hours or on High for 1 to 2 hours, or until squid is tender.

5. Add garbanzo beans and cook on Low for another 15 minutes, or until heated through. Season with salt.

The actual homeland of Swiss chard isn't in Switzerland but in the Mediterranean region. The Greek philosopher Aristotle wrote about chard in the fourth century BC, and both the ancient Greeks and Romans praised chard for its medicinal properties. Chard got its common name from another Mediterranean vegetable, cardoon, a celery-like plant with thick stalks that resemble those of chard.

Chapter 7

Veggies to Tantalize Yet Minimize

There are so many vegetables that are suitable for those on low-acid diets that you will soon be making gourmet concoctions from a variety of them on your own! Especially good is fennel, a vegetable with a white, bulbous end and green stalks and fronds. The fronds are fine for garnish, but it's the bulb you want to eat. Crunchy and clean, its taste has a hint of licorice. Long known to be good for the digestive system, it can be eaten cooked or raw.

Other especially good-for-you veggies are greens such as spinach, chard, arugula, and other lettuces; cruciferous veggies such as broccoli, cauliflower, Brussels sprouts, cabbage, kale, and collard greens; and root vegetables such as carrots, beets, and sweet potatoes. There's plenty of variety in this category, so experiment and enjoy!

Peppers Stuffed with Couscous

Flavorful and fantastic—and a beautiful presentation!

4 large red peppers

1 15-oz can cannellini beans, rinsed and drained

1 cup crumbled tofu

½ cup couscous

2 scallions, white and green parts separated, thinly sliced

1 garlic clove, minced

1 teaspoon dried oregano

Salt to taste

1. Slice a very thin layer from the base of each bell pepper so it sits flat. Slice off the tops just below the stem. Discard the stems and chop the tops, placing them in a medium bowl. Remove the ribs and seeds from the peppers.

2. In the bowl with the chopped peppers, add beans, tofu, couscous, scallion whites, garlic, and oregano. Season with salt and toss to combine.

3. Stuff the peppers with the bean mixture, and position the peppers upright in the slow cooker. Cover and cook on Low for 6 to 7 hours or on High for 3 to 4 hours.

Couscous is considered pasta because it is made from semolina, like pasta. It is believed to pre-date pasta, though, with its origins in West and North Africa, where it is still a staple. It is most associated with Moroccan cuisine.

Kale Topping

This recipe makes a little less than 2 cups of delicious kale that is great to dollop on crusty bread or add to quinoa or couscous—or to serve as a side dish to grilled meat or polenta. Consider doubling the recipe so you have it on hand.

1½ lbs kale

¼ cup olive oil

4 cloves garlic, minced

¾ cup vegetable broth

Salt to taste

1. Rinse kale and discard thick ribs and stems. Cut kale into ½-inch slices.

2. Heat oil in a deep saucepan over medium-high heat. Add garlic and cook for about 30 seconds, stirring constantly. Add kale a few handfuls at a time, and stir. Cover the pan for 30 seconds, and then stir again. Continue until all kale is wilted. Scrape kale into the slow cooker.

3. Add broth to the slow cooker, and stir well. Cover and cook on Low for 3 to 4 hours or on High for 1½ to 2 hours. Uncover and cook kale for an additional 30 to 45 minutes, or until very tender. Season with salt.

4. Dollop on crusty bread or add to quinoa or couscous, or serve as a side dish to grilled meat or polenta.

The easiest way to break apart a whole head of garlic is to slam the root end onto the countertop. It should then separate easily.

Thai Butternut Squash and Tofu

Bright, fragrant, and so very tasty, this may become a weekly extravagance!

½ cup toasted sesame seeds (toasting instructions are in the recipe)

1 tablespoons sunflower oil

1 2- to 3-lb butternut squash, peeled, seeds removed, and cut into 1-inch cubes

2 stalks celery or 1 fennel bulb, fronds removed, tough core of fennel removed, and sliced thin

2 medium carrots, peeled and sliced thin

2 thin slices raw ginger, peeled

1 stalk fresh lemon grass, peeled and cut in 2 inch pieces

½ teaspoon cumin seed

½ teaspoon turmeric

1 can light, unsweetened coconut milk

½ lb firm tofu from a block, rinsed and patted dry, then cut into ½-inch thick sticks

Fresh cilantro and/or basil leaves for garnish

1. To roast sesame seeds, spread them on a cookie sheet and put them in the oven at 275 degrees. Shake seeds around the pan frequently until seeds are a light brown color and fragrant.

2. Heat the oil in a large skillet over medium-high heat. Add the squash, celery or fennel, and carrots. Sauté for about 5 minutes, stirring constantly. Add the ginger, lemon grass, cumin seed, and turmeric, and stir for another couple of minutes. Scrape vegetable mixture into the slow cooker.

3. Add the coconut milk and stir to combine. Cover and cook on Low for 2 to 3 hours, or until vegetables are tender. Add the tofu and toasted sesame seeds, turn heat to High, cover, and cook an additional 20 to 30 minutes.

4. Serve with jasmine or basmati rice, garnishing with cilantro and/or basil.

Tofu adds protein (10 grams per half-cup serving), calcium, and iron (minerals that are especially good for women). And another reason to love it? There are only 94 calories in a half-cup, compared to more than 300 for a half-cup of either beef or cheese. What's it made out of? Plant-based soy isoflavones, which have anti-cancer benefits.

Lima Bean & Cauliflower Stew

Hearty enough to be a meal in itself, this "stew" is also an excellent choice with grilled or roasted chicken.

1½ cups dry baby lima beans

2 large carrots, peeled and diced

2 celery sticks, chopped in ¼-inch slices

1 small cauliflower, cut in large pieces

2 bay leaves

2 thin slices fresh ginger root, peeled

1 teaspoon thyme leaves

1 tablespoon olive oil

½ teaspoon ground coriander

½ teaspoon turmeric

½ teaspoon ground cumin

¼ cup minced fresh parsley

Salt to taste

1. Put the lima beans in a large bowl, add 6 cups of cold water, cover with plastic wrap, and soak overnight or for about 8 hours. If your house is hot, refrigerate the beans while soaking.

2. Drain and rinse the beans, then transfer them to a saucepot. Add water to just cover, bring the water to a boil, and skim off any foam. Turn off the heat and add the carrots and celery. Stir to combine, and add all vegetables to the slow cooker. Add water to barely cover the vegetables. Add the bay leaves, ginger slices, and thyme.

3. Cover and cook on Low for 6 to 7 hours or on High for 3 to 4 hours.

4. When nearly ready, heat the oil on low in a small frying pan, and add the coriander, turmeric, and cumin. Heat gently for a few minutes, and using a rubber spatula, transfer spices and oil to the crockpot. Add the parsley, stir to combine, and season with salt. Cover and cook for another 15 minutes on Low.

5. Just before serving, remove the ginger slices and bay leaves.

This is another great combo of ingredients for a nutrient-dense, meatless meal. Lima beans are high in fiber, rich in complex carbohydrates, packed with iron and protein, and fat free. Cauliflower is a cruciferous vegetable with antioxidant and anti-inflammatory properties, among other health benefits.

Braised Fennel

Fennel has an almost silky texture and sweet flavor once it's braised, and this side dish goes with everything. You might as well double the recipe and have more on hand.

2 medium fennel bulbs, about 1 pound each

2 tablespoons unsalted butter

½ small white onion, thinly sliced

1 clove garlic, minced

1 cup vegetable broth

2 teaspoon fresh thyme

Salt to taste

1. Cut stalks off fennel bulb, trim root end, and cut bulb in half through the root. Trim out core, then slice fennel into 1-inch thick slices across the bulb. Arrange slices in the slow cooker, and repeat with second bulb.

2. Heat butter in a small skillet over medium heat. Add onion and garlic, and cook, stirring frequently, for 3 minutes, or until onion is translucent. Scrape mixture into the slow cooker.

3. Add broth and thyme to the slow cooker. Cover and cook on Low for 4 to 6 hours or on High for 2 to 3 hours, or until fennel is tender. Season with salt, and serve hot.

> Although the celery-like stalks are trimmed off the fennel bulb for this dish, don't throw them out. They add a wonderful anise flavor as well as a crisp texture and are used in place of celery in salads and other raw dishes.

Potatoes with Herbs

This recipe features one of the best types of potatoes for people on a low-acid diet: Yukon Gold! Savor the earthiness in this easily prepared dish that is also a perfect accompaniment to everything from seafood to another vegetarian dish.

2½ lbs Yukon Gold potatoes, peeled and cut into chunks

2 medium white onions, thinly sliced

2 cloves garlic, minced

3 tablespoons unsalted butter, cut into small pieces

2 tablespoons fresh parsley, chopped

1 tablespoon fresh rosemary, chopped

1½ teaspoon fresh thyme, chopped

1½ cups low-sodium chicken broth

Salt to taste

Non-stick cooking spray

1. Spray the inside of the slow cooker liberally with non-stick cooking spray. Combine potatoes, onion, garlic, butter, parsley, rosemary, and thyme in the slow cooker. Pack it down evenly but not too firmly.

2. Poor broth over potatoes. Cover and cook on Low for 6 to 8 hours or on High for 3 to 4 hours, until potatoes are tender.

3. Season with salt and serve.

For a variation on this theme, use sweet potatoes instead of Yukon Gold potatoes. Add a teaspoon of maple syrup or brown sugar before cooking to add an extra dimension.

Toasted Barley with Mushrooms

Barley is an ancient grain that is often served in Northern Italian dishes, typically paired with beef. You'll find that the mushrooms in this recipe create a similarly rich, earthy taste and texture.

1 cup pearl barley

3 tablespoons unsalted butter

1 tablespoon olive oil

1 shallot, minced

½ lb domestic mushrooms, cleaned, caps removed, and sliced

¼ lb Portobello mushrooms, cleaned and cut into 1-inch pieces

2 cups vegetable broth

2 teaspoon fresh thyme

1 bay leaf

Salt to taste

1. Place a medium skillet over medium-high heat. Add barley and cook, stirring frequently, for 3 to 5 minutes, or until barley is lightly toasted. Transfer barley to the slow cooker.

2. Add butter and oil to the skillet. When butter melts, add shallot and mushrooms. Cook, stirring frequently, for 3 to 5 minutes, or until mushrooms begin to soften. Scrape mixture into the slow cooker.

3. Add broth, thyme, and bay leaf to the slow cooker, and stir well. Cover and cook on Low for 4 to 6 hours or on High for 2 to 3 hours, or until barley is soft. Season with salt and serve hot.

Toasting grains is an additional step for many recipes, but the results are worth it. Toasting cooks the starch on the exterior of the grain so the dish doesn't become gummy from too much starch when it cooks. Although barley is best toasted dry, any species of rice can be toasted in butter or oil. With rice, the grains just need to become opaque; they don't need to brown.

Great Green Beans

Love the texture of boiled green beans but want fresher taste? Slow cook them.

2 lbs fresh green beans

4 slices prosciutto, cut into small pieces (optional)

1 teaspoon salt

1 teaspoon garlic powder

1. Take the tips off the green beans and cut them diagonally into 1- or 2-inch pieces. If the beans aren't that fresh, cut them French style (in two down the middle).

2. Put the beans in the slow cooker, add the prosciutto pieces if desired, then season with the salt and garlic powder.

3. Add water to cover the green beans completely, but do not add too much water. Cover and cook on Low for 4 to 6 hours or on High for 2 to 3 hours, until beans are tender.

Prepare French-style beans in the same way. Instead of cutting the beans into pieces once the ends are snipped off, cut them along the seam into two long, thin strips. They'll cook the same way.

Roasted Beets

If you love beets, you'll love this method of cooking them. It "beats" waiting a long time for them to cook in boiling water!

2 bunches beets with tops (about 2 pounds)

2 tablespoons olive oil

1 clove garlic, minced

Greens from the beets, washed and cut into 1-inch pieces

Salt to taste

1. Scrub the beets clean and cut into 1-inch pieces.

2. Heat the oil in a medium skillet over medium-high heat and add the garlic. Cook, stirring constantly, about 1 minute. Add the beet greens and continue cooking and stirring until greens are just wilted, about 3 minutes.

3. Put beets into the slow cooker, topping with the greens. Cover and cook on Low for 4 to 5 hours, or on High for 3 to 4 hours, or until beets are soft.

4. Season with salt and serve.

Betacynin is the name of the pigment that gives red beets their deep color. Some people's bodies aren't able to process betacynin during digestion. As a result, their urine may be colored pink. This is temporary and is in no way harmful.

Garbanzo-Brussels Delight

The wonderful cabbage-like flavor of the Brussels sprouts is slightly sweetened by the addition of the garbanzo beans.

2 lbs Brussels sprouts

2 tablespoons olive oil

2 cloves garlic, minced

1 15-oz can garbanzo beans, drained and rinsed

¼ cup fresh parsley, chopped

Salt to taste

1. Prepare the Brussels sprouts by cutting off the coarse bottoms and removing the first few leaves, if necessary. Cut sprouts in half.

2. Heat the oil in a medium skillet over medium-high heat and add the garlic. Cook, stirring constantly, about 1 minute. Add the Brussels sprouts and continue to cook, stirring, for about 3 minutes. Transfer sprouts to the slow cooker.

3. Cover and cook on Low for 4 to 5 hours, or until sprouts are tender. Add the garbanzo beans and parsley, stir thoroughly, replace the cover, and cook an additional 15 to 20 minutes or until beans are heated through. Serve hot.

An advantage of cooking cruciferous vegetables like Brussels sprouts (or broccoli or cauliflower) in the slow cooker is that the house doesn't smell like vegetables for days, which many people find offensive. This is because very little liquid evaporates from the slow cooker, and it's the steam in the air that carries the fragrance.

Cabbage with Ginger

Slow-cooked, braised cabbage is enhanced by the slight spiciness of the fresh ginger.

1 head green cabbage, about 1 pound

2 tablespoons unsalted butter

½ small white onion, thinly sliced

1 clove garlic, minced

2 tablespoons minced, peeled fresh ginger

1 cup vegetable broth

Salt to taste

1. Cut cabbage in quarters, trim out core, then slice cabbage into 1-inch thick slices. Arrange slices in the slow cooker.

2. Heat butter in a small skillet over medium heat. Add onion and garlic, and cook, stirring frequently, for 3 minutes, or until onion is translucent. Add the ginger and cook an additional minute or so. Scrape mixture into the slow cooker.

3. Add broth to the slow cooker. Cover and cook on Low for 4 to 6 hours or on High for 2 to 3 hours, or until cabbage is tender. Season with salt, and serve hot.

This is a wonderful winter warmer and flu fighter. Cabbage helps increase your body's ability to resist infection, and ginger aids in digestion. The invigorating aroma gives a nice energy boost, too. Serve with a bowl of nutty brown rice.

Cauliflower with Potatoes and Peas

This is a classic Indian side dish, full of the flavors of fresh ginger and Indian spices.

1 tablespoon olive oil

1 small white onion, minced

1 tablespoon cumin

2 teaspoons ground coriander

1 teaspoon turmeric

1 tablespoon fresh ginger root, peeled and minced

1 small head cauliflower, separated into florets

1 medium Yukon gold potato, peeled and cubed

1 15-oz can garbanzo beans, drained and rinsed

2 cups vegetable broth

½ cup frozen peas, thawed

Salt to taste

1. Heat oil in a small skillet over medium-high heat, and add onion, cumin, coriander, and turmeric. Cook, stirring frequently, for 2 minutes, or until onion is coated with spices and they are fragrant. Turn off the flame, add the ginger, and cook an additional minute or so.

2. Scrape mixture into the slow cooker. Add cauliflower, potato, garbanzos, and vegetable broth. Cover and cook on Low for 4 to 5 hours or on High for 2 to 3 hours, or until the cauliflower and potatoes are tender.

3. Add the peas, stir to combine, replace the cover and cook an additional 15 to 20 minutes on High until peas are cooked and hot.

The spices cumin, coriander, and turmeric are absolute staples of traditional Indian cuisine. Loaded with goodness, color, and flavor, they can transform almost anything.

Black Bean Stuffed Peppers

When you load up your peppers with rice and beans, you might as well be feasting at your local *cucina*—but without the acid reflux!

2 large red peppers

2 large yellow peppers

1 15-oz can black beans, drained and rinsed

1 14-oz can corn, drained

1 cup low-sodium chicken broth

½ cup uncooked rice

½ small white onion, chopped

1 teaspoon cumin

5 oz cheddar cheese, shredded and divided

Non-stick cooking spray

1. Spray the slow cooker liberally with non-stick cooking spray.

2. Cut the peppers horizontally, and remove ribs and seeds. Position them facing up in the slow cooker.

3. In a large bowl, combine the beans, corn, broth, rice, onion, cumin, and 1 cup of the cheese; spoon into peppers.

4. Cover and cook on Low for 4 to 5 hours or on High 3 to 4 hours, or until peppers are tender and filling is heated through. Sprinkle with the remaining cheese. Cover and cook on Low for 10 minutes longer, or until cheese is melted.

If you've ever wondered why red bell peppers are always more expensive than green, it's because they are the same peppers but they've been left on the plant to mature. That's why they're sweeter and less acidic than green peppers. But they are also more perishable to ship, which accounts for their premium price.

Sweet Sweet Potatoes

Sometimes it's nice to have a vegetable dish that has a bit of sweetness to it. Besides complementing lean meats nicely, a dish like this also pairs very well with a hearty grain like barley or quinoa.

Makes 4 to 6 servings.

2 pounds sweet potatoes
¼ cup butter, cubed
¼ cup maple syrup
¼ cup packed brown sugar
Fresh basil, chopped, for garnish (optional)
Non-stick cooking spray

1. Spray the inside of the slow cooker liberally with non-stick cooking spray.

2. Put sweet potato cubes in slow cooker. In a small saucepan, combine the butter, syrup, and brown sugar and cook, stirring constantly, over medium-high heat until bubbly, about 5 minutes. Pour over potatoes.

3. Cover and cook on Low for 5 to 6 hours or on High for 2 to 3 hours, or until potatoes are tender. Before serving, drizzle with maple syrup. Garnish with basil, if you want an interesting contrast to the sweetness.

This is a side dish you will want to serve with everything from chicken to fish and even pasta dishes. Sweet potatoes are vitamin-rich and extremely versatile. You can also transfer the cooked potatoes to a bowl and mash them, stirring in a tablespoon or two of half-and-half for something really rich.

Butternut Squash and Lentils

A fabulous fall stew that's loaded with vitamins from the squash and lentils.

Makes 4 to 6 servings.

3 large stalks celery, cut into ¼-inch thick slices

1 large white onion, chopped

1 large butternut squash, peeled, seeded, and cut into 1-inch chunks

1-lb bag brown lentils

4 cups water

14- to 14.5-oz can vegetable broth

½ teaspoon dried rosemary

Salt to taste

Parmesan cheese

¼ cup loosely packed fresh parsley leaves, chopped

1. In slow cooker combine celery, onion, squash, lentils, water, broth, rosemary, and ¾ teaspoon salt.

2. Cover and cook on Low for 7 to 8 hours or on High for 4 to 6 hours, or until vegetables are tender.

3. Serve with Parmesan cheese and chopped parsley.

I love butternut squash, but even I think twice about preparing it when I know I have to peel it. It has thick skin! I was delighted when grocery stores started offering pre-peeled and cut, fresh butternut squash. What a convenience! While it doesn't have the full flavor of freshly peeled butternut squash, it is still delicious. When you want the squash without the hassle, go for the pre-peeled package.

Chapter 8

Side Dishes

That Won't Bubble Over

*S*ometimes the yummiest dishes on the table are the "sides." Intended to complement the flavors and nutrient profile of the main dish (usually a protein source like meat or fish), side dishes can vary greatly, from something primarily vegetable-based, to combinations of vegetables and starches, to simple grains or starches. It's often more entertaining for your taste buds, though, to prepare and serve several side dishes instead of limiting these delicious dishes to secondary status. With choices ranging from the heartiest of risottos to some exotic vegetable combos, like the other dishes in this collection, you'll soon want to experiment with the flavors and ingredients once you're comfortable with the slow-cooking process.

Oh-So-Good Risotto

Once you've made this Italian rice known for its porridge-like consistency in the slow cooker—without all the stirring of traditionally made risotto—you'll never do the stovetop version again!

Makes 4 servings.

3 tablespoons unsalted butter

1 medium white onion, chopped

1 cup Arborio rice

3 cups low-sodium chicken broth

½ cup Parmesan cheese

2 tablespoons fresh parsley, minced

Salt to taste

1. Heat butter in a medium saucepan over medium-high heat. Add onion and cook, stirring frequently, for 3 minutes or until onion is translucent. Add rice and stir to coat grains. Raise the heat to high and add about ¼ to ½ cup broth. Stir for about two minutes, or until it is almost evaporated. Scrape mixture into the slow cooker.

2. Add the remaining broth to the slow cooker and stir well. Cook on High for 2 hours or until rice is soft and liquid is absorbed. Stir in cheese and parsley, season with salt, and serve hot.

Risotto is one of Milan's contributions to Italian cuisine, and legend has it that it originated in the sixteenth century. True risotto alla Milanese is made with saffron, which perfumes the rice and creates a pale yellow dish. Today, almost any creamy rice dish with cheese added is called a risotto, but the authentic dish is made with Arborio rice, which, when cooked, releases a starch and creates its own sauce. The traditional dish requires constant stirring—a step happily unnecessary with the slow cooker version.

Risotto with Root Vegetables

Make this recipe in the fall and enjoy the freshness of the flavors.

Makes 4 servings.

3 tablespoons unsalted butter

1 medium white onion, chopped

1 cup Arborio rice

3 cups low-sodium chicken broth

1 cup butternut squash, peeled and cut into cubes

½ cup turnips, scrubbed clean, tops and bottoms trimmed, and cut into cubes

½ cup Parmesan cheese

Salt to taste

Fresh rosemary sprig for garnish

1. Heat butter in a medium saucepan over medium-high heat. Add onion and cook, stirring frequently, for 3 minutes or until onion is translucent. Add rice and stir to coat grains. Raise the heat to high and add about ¼ to ½ cup broth. Stir for about two minutes, or until it is almost evaporated. Scrape mixture into the slow cooker.

2. Add to the slow cooker the squash and turnips, then the remaining broth, and stir well. Cook on High for 2 to 3 hours or until rice is soft and liquid is absorbed. Stir in cheese, season with salt, and serve hot garnished with a sprig of rosemary.

Rosemary is a delightful accompaniment to the flavors of this risotto. As a garnish it has great visual appeal; for additional flavor, peel some leaves off a stem and chop them fine, sprinkling them into the rice before serving.

Melt in Your Mouth Mushroom Risotto

If you love mushrooms, you will love this dish—and you'll come to crave it for its total satisfaction!

Makes 4 servings.

3 tablespoons unsalted butter

1 medium white onion, chopped

1 cup Arborio rice

2½ cups low-sodium chicken broth

1 cup domestic mushrooms, trimmed and sliced

1 cup Portobello mushrooms, cut into 1-inch cubes

½ cup Parmesan cheese

Sprig of thyme for garnish

Salt to taste

1. Heat butter in a medium saucepan over medium-high heat. Add onion and cook, stirring frequently, for 3 minutes or until onion is translucent. Add rice and stir to coat grains. Raise the heat to high and add about ¼ to ½ cup broth. Stir for about two minutes, or until it is almost evaporated. Scrape mixture into the slow cooker.

2. In the skillet, add the mushrooms and sauté in the oil that sticks to the pan for about 2 minutes or until the mushrooms are just soft, stirring constantly.

3. Add the mushrooms to the slow cooker, then the remaining broth, and stir well. Cook on High for 2 to 3 hours or until rice is soft and liquid is absorbed. Stir in cheese, season with salt, and serve hot. Garnish with sprig of thyme.

Arborio rice is uniquely Italian and is named after the town in which it was developed. It is a short, fat grain with a pearly white exterior and high starch content, the result of less milling. Another of its characteristics is its ability to absorb flavors.

Barley Risotto

If you enjoy the risotto recipes with traditional Arborio rice, try this one made with barley for a change. It introduces additional nuttiness and nutrients.

Makes 4 servings.

1 tablespoon unsalted butter

1 medium leek, white and light green parts only, thinly sliced

½ cup Portobello mushrooms, cubed

5¼ cups low-sodium chicken broth

1½ cups pearled barley (10½ oz), rinsed

1 carrot, peeled and thinly sliced

1 sprig thyme

¼ cup freshly grated Parmesan cheese, plus more for serving

Salt to taste

1. Heat butter in a medium saucepan over medium-high heat. Add leeks and mushrooms and cook, stirring frequently, for 3 minutes or until onion is translucent and mushrooms have softened.

2. In a slow cooker, combine the barley, carrots, and sprig of thyme. Add the onion/mushroom mixture and the chicken broth and stir to combine.

3. Cover and cook on Low for 3 to 4 hours, until the liquid is absorbed.

4. Before serving, discard the thyme sprig and stir in the cheese and butter. Season with salt to taste. Serve hot, with additional Parmesan if desired.

> Pearled barley is barley that has had its hull removed and the inner grain polished or "pearled." Most grains have their hulls removed, as they can't be digested, and this requires processing. Look for regular-sized grains of pearled barley, as the smaller the grains get the more processing is involved.

Herbed Polenta

Polenta hails from Italy, though it wasn't developed until corn started coming in from the New World. It's a corn "oatmeal" of sorts, and in this country it's most often cooked up for breakfast in place of grits, though it's developing more and more of a following in culinary circles.

Makes 4 servings.

5 cups low-sodium chicken broth

1 cup low-fat milk

1 cup polenta (yellow corn meal)

½ teaspoon fresh parsley, chopped

½ teaspoon fresh thyme, chopped

½ teaspoon fresh rosemary, chopped

3 tablespoons unsalted butter

1 cup grated cheddar

Salt to taste

Non-stick cooking spray

1. Spray the inside of the slow cooker liberally with non-stick cooking spray. Combine the broth, milk, and polenta in the slow cooker. Whisk together thoroughly, cover, and cook on High for about 1½ hours, or until mixture begins to boil.

2. Add the herbs to the slow cooker. Whisk again, cover, and cook on High an additional 1½ hours, then turn heat to Low and cook for 2 or 3 more hours, or until polenta is very thick.

3. Stir in the butter and cheese, and season with salt. Serve hot.

An alternative way to serve polenta is to pack the hot polenta into a well-oiled loaf pan and chill it well. Once chilled you can cut it into slices and either grill or sauté them in butter or olive oil. You can also spread the polenta in a shallow baking dish to the thickness of ¾ inch, and then chill the mixture, cut it into long, narrow rectangles, and pan-fry them.

Indian Rice

The fragrant cumin and turmeric in this dish will awaken all your senses. It's delicious with almost any chicken dish.

Makes 6 servings.

4 cups brown rice

½ teaspoon ground cumin

½ teaspoon turmeric

3 tablespoons butter, cut into small pieces

4 cups low-sodium chicken broth

4 cups water

Non-stick cooking spray

1. Spray the inside of the slow cooker liberally with non-stick cooking spray. Add the rice and spices to the slow cooker, and stir to combine. Put the pieces of butter over the rice, then add the broth and water.

2. Cover and cook on Low for 4 to 6 hours or on High for 2 to 3 hours. To keep rice from drying out too much or burning, check it about an hour before it should be ready, and if it's looking good, turn the cooker to Warm. It can cook through on Warm for several hours. Serve hot.

Brown rice is simply rice that has not been polished to remove the bran layer, as is done to produce white rice. Because only the hull is removed and the bran layer and germ are retained, brown rice has a nuttier flavor and chewier texture than white rice. It also has more vitamins, minerals, and fiber, as those are concentrated in the bran layer.

Sweet Potato and Tofu

The textures of these two foods work well together, and the drizzle of maple syrup gives the dish a special touch.

Makes 4 servings.

2 large sweet potatoes, peeled and cut into cubes

1 lb firm tofu, rinsed and cut into cubes

½ cup chicken or vegetable broth

½ teaspoon thyme, dried

½ teaspoon rosemary, dried

¼ or ½ cup natural maple syrup, to taste

Non-stick cooking spray

1. Spray the inside of the slow cooker liberally with non-stick spray. Put in the sweet potato and tofu cubes and mix together. Add the broth and the herbs, and stir to combine.

2. Cook on Low 4 to 5 hours or on High 2 to 3 hours, until potatoes and tofu are cooked through. Before serving, drizzle maple syrup over the mix. Serve hot.

Tofu originated in China in approximately 960 AD. It is made through a process of curding soymilk. Today it is the most widely used soy food in the world. In Asia, it is as important as meat, cheese, and milk are to us here in the West.

Brown Rice and Mixed Vegetables

This is a super-simple way to prepare rice with nutritious vegetables.

Makes 6 servings.

4 cups brown rice

1 10-oz package of frozen mixed vegetables or 1 large can or 2 small cans of vegetables of your choice

3 tablespoons butter, cut into small pieces

4 cups low-sodium chicken broth

4 cups water

Non-stick cooking spray

1. Spray the inside of the slow cooker liberally with non-stick cooking spray. Add the rice to the slow cooker. Add vegetables and stir to combine. Put the pieces of butter over the rice, then add the broth and water.

2. Cover and cook on Low for 4 to 6 hours or on High for 2 to 3 hours. To keep rice from drying out too much or burning, check it about an hour before it should be ready, and if it's looking good, turn the cooker to Warm. It can cook through on Warm for several hours.

The variations on this dish are many. Simply swap out a package of traditional mixed vegetables for another vegetable, such as broccoli florets, broccoli and cauliflower, corn niblets, Asian-themed vegetables, and so on. Be sure to choose vegetables that are not sauced in any way.

Bulgur Pilaf with Broccoli and Carrots

This super-nutritious and super-simple dish is delicious by itself or as an accompaniment to a simple meat or fish dish.

Makes 4 servings.

2 cups uncooked bulgur wheat
or cracked wheat

1 tablespoon butter, melted

1 teaspoon salt

4 medium carrots, peeled and cut
into thin slices

1 white onion, chopped

3½ cups vegetable or chicken broth

4 cups chopped fresh broccoli, cut
into florets, toughest stems removed

1 cup shredded cheddar cheese

Non-stick cooking spray

1. Spray the slow cooker liberally with the non-stick cooking spray.

2. Put the bulgur, butter, salt, carrots, onion, and broth into the slow cooker and stir to combine. Cover and cook on Low for 6 to 8 hours or on High for 3 to 4 hours, turning the heat to Low for another hour or so, or until bulgur is tender.

3. Stir in the broccoli and cheese. Increase the heat to High, cover, and cook an additional 15 to 20 minutes until the broccoli is tender and the cheese is melted through. Serve hot.

> Bulgur is a whole wheat grain that has been cracked and partially pre-cooked. Because it is a whole grain, it is low in fat and high in fiber.

Scalloped Potatoes

Once you have the potatoes peeled and sliced, it's just a matter of stacking them in the slow cooker, adding the other ingredients, and returning to a masterpiece.

Makes 4 to 6 servings.

6 medium Idaho potatoes, thinly sliced

1 white onion, thinly sliced

1 cup low-fat shredded cheddar cheese

½ cup fresh parsley, minced

10 domestic mushrooms, cleaned and thinly sliced

½ cup low-fat milk

½ cup butter, melted

½ teaspoon paprika

Salt to taste

Non-stick cooking spray

1. Spray the inside of the slow cooker liberally with non-stick cooking spray. In the slow cooker, alternate layers of potatoes, onions, cheese, parsley, and mushrooms until all are used up.

2. In a small bowl, combine the milk, butter, paprika, and salt. Pour this mixture over the ingredients in the slow cooker.

3. Cover and cook on Low for 7 to 9 hours or on High for 3 to 4 hours until potatoes are cooked through and bubbly. Serve hot.

This dish is classically prepared with heavy cream and lots of butter. While this makes an especially creamy dish, scalloped potatoes can be just as satisfying with far less fat and calories, as this recipe proves. The slow cooking renders the thinly sliced potatoes tender and tasty.

Veggie Stew with Tofu

Pile your plate high with the many vegetables included in this tasty recipe! Serve with rice or crusty French bread.

Makes 4 to 6 servings.

1 lb extra firm tofu

2 cups broccoli florets

2 cups cauliflower florets

2 Idaho potatoes, scrubbed, peeled, and diced

1 white onion, minced

1 clove garlic, minced

2 carrots, peeled and sliced

1½ cups vegetable stock

2 teaspoon thyme, dried

2 teaspoon sage, dried

2 tablespoons fresh parsley, chopped

1 bay leaf

1 14-oz can yellow or white corn

1 14-oz can sweet baby peas

Salt to taste

1. Prepare tofu by rinsing the block and cutting it into small, bite-sized cubes.

2. In a large bowl, combine the broccoli, cauliflower, potatoes, onion, garlic, and carrots. Stir to combine, and add to slow cooker. Cover with stock. Add tofu and add herbs, and stir again to combine.

3. Cover and cook on Low for 6 to 8 hours or on High for 4 to 5 hours. In the last hour of cooking, add the canned vegetables and stir to combine. Continue cooking until vegetables are tender. Serve hot.

> Most recipes call for broccoli florets, which often leaves cooks with large broccoli stems. Don't toss them! With a paring knife, peel off the tough outer skin and cut off the woodiest parts, especially the bottom of the stem. The rest is crunchy, tasty broccoli. Cut it into rounds or strips and munch away, or save it for salads.

Exotic Eggplant and Chickpeas

If you want to dress up a simple fish dish with a vegetable side that has a fragrant spice and a rich flavor, try this one.

Makes 4 servings.

1 tablespoon olive oil

1 white onion, chopped

3 cloves garlic, minced

1 large eggplant, cubed

1 cup cauliflower florets, if desired

½ teaspoon cumin

¼ teaspoon cinnamon

1 15-oz can chickpeas, drained and rinsed

1 cup vegetable broth

2 cups water

Salt to taste

1. Heat oil in a medium skillet over medium-high heat. Add onion and garlic and cook for 2 to 3 minutes, until onion is translucent. Add eggplant and cauliflower and continue cooking another minute or two until vegetables just begin to heat up. Turn off the heat and stir in the cumin and cinnamon. Scrape mixture into the slow cooker.

2. Add the chickpeas, broth, and water, and season lightly with salt. Cover and cook on Low for 6 to 7 hours or on High for 4 to 5 hours, or until vegetables are tender. Serve hot.

There are two reasons why eggplant is salted before cooking. The first is to draw out the innate bitterness and the other is to draw out some of the water so that it sautés more easily. While this is necessary with large eggplants, it can be skipped if using thin Japanese eggplants (which aren't bitter).

Chapter 9

Dessert Without Hurt

One of the toughest parts of any "diet" is cutting back on or eliminating sweets. When you start paying close attention to ingredients—especially of prepackaged foods in the grocery store—you'll be amazed at how many of them contain sugar or some form of sugar. While sugar isn't a reflux trigger, it is advisable to try to limit or abstain from it for an optimally healthy diet. Brown sugar and all-natural maple syrup are preferable to refined sugar, and the ingredients in these recipes reflect that. Just as over time you may have been able to reduce the amount of sugar you added to coffee or tea, so, too, can you start to reduce the amount of sugar in your overall diet. All that said, a tasty dessert is an indulgence that is worth it, so this is a necessary chapter.

And remember, while adding fruit adds flavor (and great nutrients), not all fruits are low-acid. Indulge in melon, bananas, pears, and raspberries. Avoid citrus fruits, blueberries, pineapple, cranberries, pomegranate, mango, and the apple varietals Granny Smith, Macoun, and Macintosh. If you're uncertain, remember the higher the pH, the better.

Rice Pudding

Once you master this simple recipe, you can add fruits and flavorings to it. Its creamy goodness makes it taste like it's more calories than it is.

Makes 4 servings.

¾ cup long-grain white rice

3 cups low-fat milk

½ cup dark brown sugar

½ teaspoon ground cinnamon

1 pinch salt

1 cardamom pod

100% natural maple syrup to drizzle on top

1. Place rice in a colander, and rinse it well under cold water.

2. Grease the inside of the slow cooker liberally with vegetable oil spray. Spoon rice into the slow cooker.

3. Combine the milk with the brown sugar, cinnamon, and salt. Stir. Add the cardamom pod. Carefully pour the milk mixture on top of the rice, and stir to combine.

4. Cook on Low for 4 to 5 hours or on High for 2 to 3 hours, or until rice has absorbed the liquid. Remove the cardamom pod, turn off the heat, and let sit for a half-hour or so. Serve warm with a drizzle of maple syrup.

Cardamom is an ancient spice originating in India and the Middle East. Pods keep the flavor the freshest and are best for cooking. Cardamom lends an aromatic, citrusy undertone to dishes. While it is distinct on its own, it can be substituted with a combination of cinnamon and nutmeg. Since there's already cinnamon in this recipe, you could add ¼ teaspoon nutmeg instead of the cardamom.

Raspberry-Pear Cobbler

Raspberry season falls in some of the hottest months, when it would be great to make cobbler or shortcake, but you don't want to turn on your oven. Here's the solution: the slow cooker! The addition of pears mellows the raspberries just a touch and adds texture.

Makes 4 servings.

1 cup all-purpose flour

¾ cup brown sugar

1 teaspoon baking powder

¼ teaspoon salt

¼ teaspoon ground cinnamon

¼ teaspoon ground nutmeg

2 eggs, lightly beaten

3 tablespoons vegetable oil

2 tablespoons low-fat milk

4 cups fresh or frozen raspberries

2 cups fresh or frozen Bosc pears, cored and cut into cubes

1 cup water

3 tablespoons quick-cooking tapioca

½ cup maple syrup

1. In a medium bowl, stir together flour, ¾ cup brown sugar, baking powder, salt, cinnamon, and nutmeg. In a small bowl, combine eggs, oil, and milk. Add egg mixture all at once to flour mixture. Stir just until moistened. Set aside.

2. In a large saucepan, combine berries and pears, the water, and tapioca. Bring to a boil. Add maple syrup to hot fruit mixture, remove from heat, and put into the slow cooker. Immediately spoon the batter over the fruit mixture.

3. Cover and cook on Low for 4 to 5 hours or on High for 1 to 2 hours. Test for doneness by inserting a toothpick in the center. If it comes out clean, it's done. When done, turn the cooker off, leave uncovered, and let stand for about 30 minutes to cool. Serve warm.

> Cooking the fruits with the tapioca before adding them to the slow cooker intensifies their flavor and also helps reduce the amount of liquid they give off while cooking.

Indian Pudding

This thick and rich pudding is a wonderful fall or winter dessert, rich with maple syrup and brown sugar.

Makes 4 servings.

5 cups low-fat milk

¼ cup firmly packed brown sugar

½ cup maple syrup

¾ cup yellow cornmeal (organic is best)

6 tablespoons unsalted butter

¼ teaspoon vanilla extract

1 teaspoon fresh ginger root

Pinch of salt

Non-stick cooking spray

1. Combine milk, brown sugar, and maple syrup in a 2-quart saucepan, and stir well. Heat over medium heat, stirring occasionally, until mixture comes to a boil. Whisk in cornmeal and simmer mixture, whisking frequently, for about 10 minutes or until thick.

2. Stir butter and vanilla into the mix, and whisk until butter melts. Remove the pan from the heat. Stir in the ginger and pinch of salt.

3. Spray the inside of the slow cooker with non-stick cooking spray. Using a spatula, transfer all of the pudding mixture into the slow cooker. Cover and cook on Low for 3 to 5 hours. (Do not cook on High.)

4. When the edges have darkened slightly and the center is set, the pudding is done. Turn off the cooker, uncover, and let cool until warm. Serve.

Because Native Americans introduced corn to the Pilgrims, anything made with corn had "Indian" as a prefix at one time or another. The other term for Indian Pudding is Hasty Pudding, and the Hasty Puddng Club at Harvard University, founded in 1770, was named for the dessert because it was eaten at the first meeting. Recipes for Indian or Hasty pudding go back to the early eighteenth century.

Banana Bomb Cake

This is a decadent dessert for a special occasion. This recipe calls for imitation rum extract, which contains about 29% alcohol by volume. While alcohol is an unwise choice for a low-acid diet, the alcohol in the extract is a stabilizer. The volume in the overall recipe is minimal (1 tablespoon), and part of the alcohol itself burns off in the cooking.

Makes 4 to 6 servings.

2 tablespoons butter, softened, for greasing the aluminum foil

¾ cup firmly packed brown sugar

1 tablespoon imitation rum extract (for flavoring)

1 tablespoon water

6 medium-sized, ripe bananas, peeled and sliced into circles

¾ cup flour

¾ teaspoon baking powder

¼ teaspoon salt

½ teaspoon cinnamon

¼ teaspoon nutmeg

4 tablespoons butter

1¼ cups sugar

1 whole egg, and 1 egg separated (yolk only)

2 tablespoons low-fat milk

Frozen vanilla yogurt (optional; for serving on the cake)

Non-stick cooking spray

Aluminum foil

1. Spray the inside of the slow cooker with non-stick cooking spray. Line the entire slow cooker with aluminum foil (sides can extend over the top). Grease the aluminum foil with a tablespoon or two of the butter, softened, so it is covered thoroughly.

2. Sprinkle the brown sugar over the bottom of the slow cooker. Drizzle the imitation rum and water over the sugar. Position the bananas over the sugar, pressing them in securely but without squishing them. Turn the cooker to High and leave uncovered while you prepare the cake.

3. In a large bowl, combine flour, baking powder, salt, cinnamon, and nutmeg. Use a whisk to combine the ingredients thoroughly.

4. In a medium-sized bowl, use an electric mixer to beat the butter and sugar until just blended, then beat on high speed until the mixture is light and fluffy. Add the whole egg and beat on a lower speed until combined. Add the egg yolk and beat until combined.

5. With the beaters on low or medium, begin adding the flour mixture. Working in batches, beat in about ⅓ of the flour, then 1 tablespoon milk, more flour, milk, and ending with the flour.

6. When the batter is smooth, pour it over the bananas and sugar in the slow cooker. Using a double layer of paper towels, cover the top of the cooker before fitting it with the actual cover. This will create a tighter seal and help absorb excess liquid.

7. Cover securely and let cook on High for 3 to 4 hours, or until edges are slightly browned and the cake is springy to the touch. Turn off the cooker and let rest for about 15 minutes.

8. Lift the cake from the slow cooker using the aluminum foil. Allow to cool out of the cooker for about half an hour, then invert onto a plate before serving so bananas are showing.

9. Serve with a scoop of frozen vanilla yogurt while the cake is still warm.

Full of Fall Cake

This moist cake is a great treat any time of year, but especially in the fall months.

Makes 6 servings.

3 cups unsweetened chunky apple sauce

2 cups flour

1 cup brown sugar

¼ cup maple syrup

1 cup canned pumpkin

3 eggs, beaten

⅓ cup vegetable oil

2 teaspoons baking powder

¼ teaspoon baking soda

Pinch salt

1 teaspoon cinnamon

¼ teaspoon nutmeg

Non-stick cooking spray

1. Liberally spray the inside of the slow cooker with non-stick cooking spray. Put applesauce in bottom and spread evenly to cover.

2. In a large bowl, combine flour, brown sugar, syrup, pumpkin, eggs, vegetable oil, baking powder, baking soda, salt, and spices. Beat with electric mixer on medium until combined, and then for another 2 minutes, scraping the sides of the bowl. Use a spatula to transfer the cake mixture to the slow cooker and over the applesauce mixture.

3. Double layer some paper towels and place over the top of the cooker to absorb any additional moisture. Cover the slow cooker as usual, and cook on High for 2 hours or until a toothpick inserted in the center comes out clean. Serve cake warm with plain or frozen yogurt if desired.

You could dress up this cake even more with the addition of unsweetened, flaked coconut. Stir in about ½ cup just before you add the cake to the slow cooker.

Table of Weights and Measures of Common Ingredients

FOOD	QUANTITY	YIELD
Apples	1 pound	2$\frac{1}{2}$ to 3 cups sliced
Bananas	1 medium	1 cup, sliced
Bell Peppers	1 pound	3 to 4 cups sliced
Broccoli	1 head	3 to 4 cups, chopped
Butter	$\frac{1}{4}$ pound (1 stick)	8 tablespoons
Cabbage	1 pound	4 cups packed shredded
Carrots	1 pound	3 cups diced or sliced
Cauliflower	1 head	4 to 6 cups, chopped
Fennel	1 head	2 cups chopped, fronds removed
Flour, rice	1 pound	4 cups
Milk	1 quart	4 cups
Mushrooms	1 pound	5 cups sliced
Onions	1 medium	$\frac{1}{2}$ cup chopped
Potatoes	1 pound	3 cups sliced
Raisins	1 pound	3 cups
Rice	1 pound	2 to 2$\frac{1}{2}$ cups raw
Spinach	1 pound	$\frac{3}{4}$ cup cooked
Squash, summer	1 pound	3$\frac{1}{2}$ cups sliced
Sugar, brown	1 pound	2$\frac{1}{4}$ cups, packed

Index

Dominique DeVito has been in publishing for over 20 years, and has written books on everything from decorating to beekeeping to pet care. Of French descent, she has been experimenting in the kitchen since she was young, and works closely with chefs and caterers as part of her current venture as co-owner of the Hudson-Chatham Winery in Ghent, New York, where she lives with her family.

Breea Johnson is a Registered Dietician (RD) and Licensed Dietician Nutritionist (LDN) in Chicago, where she has a private practice, Sustaining Nutrition: Integrative Nutrition Counseling. Her nutrition-related projects have included a study on probiotics and gastrointestinal symptoms at Hines Veterans Administration Hospital. She is dedicated to giving people tools—including delicious recipes—to help them achieve better health through diet.

About Cider Mill Press
Book Publishers

Good ideas ripen with time. From seed to harvest, Cider Mill Press brings fine reading, information, and entertainment together between the covers of its creatively crafted books. Our Cider Mill bears fruit twice a year, publishing a new crop of titles each spring and fall.

Visit us on the Web at
www.cidermillpress.com
or write to us at
12 Port Farm Road
Kennebunkport, Maine 04046